365
WONDERS
OF THE
WORLD

Edited by: Tapasi de

Designed by: Rakesh Kumar

2st Impression

© B. Jain Publishers (P) Ltd.

Published by
Kuldeep Jain
for
Pegasus
An imprint of
B. Jain Publishers (P) Ltd.
An ISO 9001 : 2000 Certified Company
1921, Street No. 10, Chuna Mandi, Paharganj, New Delhi-110055 (INDIA)
Tel: 91-11-4567 1000 | Fax: 91-11-4567 1010
Website: **www.pegasusforkids.com** | E-mail: **info@bjain.com**

ISBN: 978-81-319-3252-0

Printed in India by Gopsons Papers Ltd

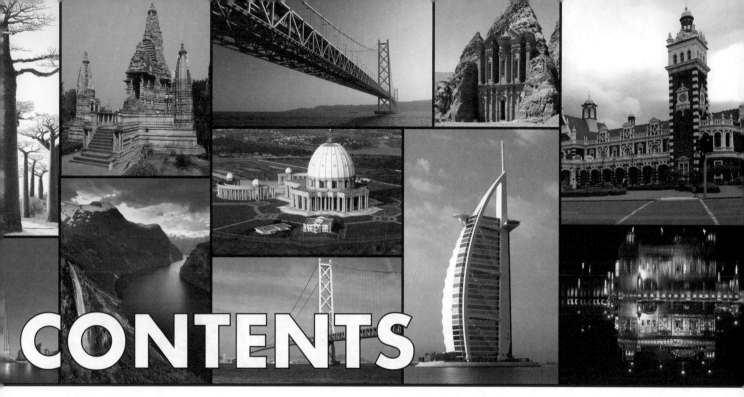

CONTENTS

North America (Natural Wonders)

1 Avenue of the Baobab

The **Avenue or Alley of the Baobabs** is an extraordinary group of baobab trees lining a dirt road in western Madagascar. Its visually mesmerising landscape draws tourists from all around the world. Along the road are about a dozen trees about 30 m in height, of the species **Adansonia grandidieri**, which is only found in Madagascar. These Baobab trees are up to 800 years old!

2 Canary Islands

The **Canary Islands** which lie off the north-west coast of Morocco, are tips of a volcanic mountain range. The topography of the islands is incredibly varied. The seven main islands of the Canary Islands are well spaced out.

The beaches, climate and important natural attractions make it a unique tourist spot. It is especially for Maspalomas in Gran Canaria, Teide National Park and Mount Teide (the third tallest volcano in the world measured from its base on the ocean floor), that make it a major tourist destination with over 12 million visitors per year.

3 Eye of Sahara

The Richat Structure, also known as the **Eye of the Sahara** or **blue eye of Africa**, is a strange and prominent geological circular feature in the Sahara Desert. It is nearly 50 kilometres across in diameter and even visible from space!

Initially, scientists thought that this unique geological phenomenon was an asteroid impact structure because of its circular shape. But now it is thought to be a highly symmetrical and deeply eroded geologic dome that has collapsed. But the fact that the 'rings', are equidistant from the centre and that the structure is nearly circular in shape, still remains a mystery.

4 Krugar National Park

Lying in the heart of the Lowveld is a wildlife sanctuary **Krugar National Park**. It is the largest game reserve in South Africa, larger even than Israel. It consists of nearly 2 million hectares of land that stretch for 352 km from north to south along the Mozambique border. Visiting Krugar, is considered to be the most incredible wildlife experience.

Its plant life includes baobabs, fever trees, knob thorns, marulas and mopane trees. Animals include lions, elephants, cape buffaloes, leopards, rhinos, buffalo and rare insects like antlion and rhine beetle.

5 Lake Nakuru

The word Nakuru means 'dust or dusty place' in Maasai language. **Lake Nakuru National Park**, close to Nakuru town, was established in 1961. Lake Nakuru, is a small, shallow alkaline lake which lies about 160 km north of Nairobi. The lake is well-known as myriads of fuschia pink flamingoes, often more than a million, flock there. They feed on the abundant algae, which thrives in the warm waters.

A UNESCO Heritage Site, Lake Nakuru National Park is also home to hippos, white and black rhino, giraffe and buffalo.

6 Lake Turkana National Park

Turkana, the most saline of Africa's large lakes, is an outstanding laboratory for the study of plant and animal species in Kenya. **Lake Turkana National Parks** are constituted of Sibiloi National Park, the South Island and the Central Island National Parks.

These three National Parks are a resting point for migrant water birds. The site is also the important breeding grounds for Nile crocodile, hippopotamus and a range of poisonous snakes.

7 Mt. Kilimanjaro

Kilimanjaro, with its three volcanic cones, Kibo, Mawenzi, and Shira, is a dormant volcanic mountain in Kilimanjaro National Park, Tanzania. It is the highest mountain in Africa and the highest free-standing mountain in the world at 5,895 m above sea level. Interestingly, Kilimanjaro is one of the world's most accessible high summits. This is probably the reason it attracts visitors from around the world. Most climbers reach the crater rim with a walking stick, proper clothing and determination. And those who reach Uhuru Point, the actual summit, or Gillman's Point on the lip of the crater, earn certificates for climbing.

8 Ngorongoro Crater

Ngorongoro Crater in Tanzania is the world's largest unbroken caldera. It is often referred to as 'Africa's Garden of Eden'. Ngorongoro Crater was created from a volcano that exploded creating the caldera. The crater is 19 km wide and covers 264 sq km of wilderness. The rim of the crater rises just over 610 m above the caldera floor reaching an elevation of 2,286 m.

The crater shelters over 30,000 animals including elephants, lions, cheetahs, wildebeests, buffaloes, and the rare black rhinos. There are few places on earth where such a tremendous diversity of landscapes exist inside a region this size! This unique crater is also of great archaeological importance, as the remains of some of mankind's earliest ancestors have been discovered in this area.

9 Okavango Delta

The **Okavango Delta** is the world's largest inland delta and is situated in an extremely arid region that shelters great concentrations of diverse animals and birds. It spans over 16,000 square kilometres. It is one of the most incredible travel destinations with its lush green environment. The Okavango Delta is situated deep within the Kalahari Basin, and is often called the 'jewel' of the Kalahari.

The Delta which is a watery labyrinth of narrow canals that are best navigated by Mokoro, a traditional dugout canoe. The Okavango Delta is fed by the Okavango River. In a country most of which is arid, the Delta is a permanent life giving waterway.

10 River Nile

The **River Nile** is about 6,670 km in length and is the longest river in Africa and in the world! It was by the banks of this mighty river that one of the oldest civilizations in the world began.

Most of Ancient Egypt's historical sites are located along the banks of the Nile River including cities such as Luxor and Cairo.

This great river drains into the Mediterranean Sea in the Nile Delta in Northern Egypt. The Aswan High Dam was built in 1970 to help regulate flooding of the Nile River. The felucca (a typical boat) still serves as the primary transportation over the centuries on the Nile.

The Nile is full of many water creatures and crocodiles are very common along its banks. Fishing Eagles are a common bird along the Nile.

11 Sahara Desert

The **Sahara Desert** in the continent of Africa is the largest hot desert in the world. It covers most of Northern Africa, making it almost as large as Europe or the United States! Due to the high temperatures and arid conditions of Sahara, plant life is sparse. There are barely 70 different animal species. Some of them are gerbil, sand fox, cape hare, sand viper and the monitor lizard.

The Sahara Desert covers 11 countries in its expanse — the countries of Algeria, Chad, Egypt, Libya, Mali, Mauritania, Morocco, Niger, Western Sahara, Sudan, and Tunisia.

The landscape of the desert includes huge sand dunes and dune fields.

12 Serengeti Migration

The **Serengeti** region in north-western Tanzania spans some 30,000 square km and hosts the largest and longest migration in the world.

Sometimes during the month of October, when the plains have dried after the rain, almost 2 million herbivore animals along with the wildebeest move west towards Lake Victoria in search of pasture and rains. Following the rainfalls the migration moves on to the north, into the Masai Mara. With the start of the monsoon rains in December, the wildebeest move back into the green Serengeti plains. This phenomenon is sometimes called the 'circular migration'.

13 Siwa Oasis

In the Western Desert close to the Libyan border lies Egypt's most remote oasis town, **Siwa**. This isolated oasis has natural springs and fertile land.

Siwans speak their own language and their jewellery and crafts are extraordinary. A decent road and a small airport have certainly attracted tourist from all over the globe. History says that Alexander the Great travelled here to visit the Oracle of Amun.

It's a wonderful place to relax, swim and eat some olives. The old town of Siwa dates back to the 13th century.

It's a great spot for gazing from your tent towards the sand, and also taking a dip in its hot and cold natural pools.

14 Table Mountain

The **Table Mountain** is located in the Western Cape in South Africa. It is 1,087 m high. It stands over Cape Town and the Table Bay. The amusing thing about it is that its peak is flat. Sometimes a dense white mist covers its top and gives it an appearance of a 'tablecloth.'

The Table Mountain is believed to be one of the oldest mountains in the world.

It has over 1,500 species of plants, more than those found in the entire United Kingdom! A 65-passenger cable car runs from Tafelberg Road to the top of the Table Mountain. The floor rotates giving everyone a 360 degree view on the way up. The cable cars take about 5-10 minutes to reach the top of the mountain.

15 Tsingy de Bemaraha Strict Nature Reserv

Tsingy de Bemaraha Reserve is located in the drier eastern side of Madagascar. It has a distinct fauna and flora on a karst landscape. The place is full of spiky limestone rock formations ranging upto 100 m and mangrove forests. The forests forms the home of many rare and endangered species.

16 Victoria Falls

The **Victoria Falls** (locally called **Mosi-oa-Tunya** meaning 'the smoke that thunders') is a waterfall located in southern Africa on the Zambezi River between the countries of Zambia and Zimbabwe. The whole river drops headlong from a height of 108 m spanning the full one-and-a-half kilometre width of the river.

The Victoria Falls is neither the highest nor the widest waterfall in the world. It is however the largest. This claim is based on a width of 1,708 m and height of 108 m which forms the biggest curtain of falling water in the world and also one of the seven natural wonders of the world. Victoria Falls is roughly twice the height of North America's Niagara Falls and more than twice the width of Horseshoe Falls.

The fall is so great that the spray from the falls normally rises to a height of over 400 m and sometimes even 800 m. Close to the edge of the cliff, spray shoots upward like inverted rain! This spray is visible from up to a distance of 50 km!

17 Vredefort Dome

Vredefort Dome, which is 120 km south west of Johannesburg, is a large meteorite impact structure or astrobleme. It dates back to 2,023 million years! It is the oldest astrobleme found on earth so far. It has a radius of 190 km; it is also the largest and the most deeply eroded. Till date, it is the site of the world's greatest single, known energy release event.

AFRICA (Manmade Wonders)

18 Abu Simbel

In 1257 BCE, Pharaoh Ramses II got two temples carved out of solid rocks on the west bank of the Nile, south of Aswan in the land of Nubia. This place today is known as **Abu Simbel**. It was shifted to a higher ground in the 1960s as the water of Lake Nasser began to rise following the completion of the Aswan dam. Abu Simbel faces east, and Re-Horakhty, one manifestation of the Sun God, is shown inside the niche directly above the entrance. The temple has been aligned in such a manner that twice a year the Sun's rays reach into the innermost part of the temple to illuminate the seated statues of Ptah, Amun-

Re, Ramesses II and Re-Horakhty. This ancient temple has been included in the UNESCO World Heritage Site.

19 Basilica Notre Dame de la Paix

Basilica Notre Dame de la Paix, which is also known as 'Basilica of Our Lady of Peace of Yammousoukro' is considered to be the tallest and largest church in the whole world. The construction of this basilica started in 1985 and was completed 4 years later. It costed $300 million to complete the basilica. The design of Basilica Notre Dame de la Paix was inspired by Rome's Basilica of Saint Peter. It has an awestriking seating capacity of 7,000 people! Fine marble from Italy and stained glass from France have been used for construction.

20 Egyptian Museum

The **Egyptian Museum** was begun by the Egyptian government in 1835 to control the looting of Egypt's priceless artifacts. The museum located in Cairo began in 1858 with a collection gathered by Auguste Mariette, the French archaeologist retained by Isma'il Pasha.

This world famous museum houses 120,000 artifacts. It has an incredible display of mummies, sarcophagi, pottery, jewellery and of course King Tutankhamen's treasures.

Pharaoh Tutankhamen's tomb collection forms the major highlight of this museum. The tomb of Tutankhamen (better known as 'King Tut') was found remarkably intact by Howard Carter in the Valley of the Kings in 1923. The 'Mummy Room', houses 11 royal mummies from pharaonic times. This room has an entrance fee and does not allow photography.

21 Ganvie

Ganvie is a unique village built on Lake Nokoué in Benin, West Africa. It is just an hour away from Benin's largest city, Cotonou. Approximately, 20,000 people live in Ganvie. It's commonly believed that the Tofinu people settled here around 400 years ago and built their lake village with a specific purpose. It was to escape slavers who came from the Fon tribe and were not allowed to fight in water for traditional reasons or maybe they could not swim.

Most of the people of this matchless settlement rely on fishing and tourism for their living. Most tourists spent their time floating around taking photographs and observing the daily life.

22 Great Sphinx

The great ancient structure of **Sphinx** in Giza remains the epitome of mystery. It is a large human-headed lion that was carved from a mound of limestone. The Sphinx was built around 2530 BC by the Pharaoh Khafre. This mysterious structure is thought to be guarding the pyramids by warding off evil spirits since the last 4000 years! It is believed that the Ancient Egyptians worshipped the Sphinx and offered sacrifices to it. They also left messages on stone tablets which have been discovered.

23 Karnak Temple

The **Karnak Temple** is a vast temple complex in Luxor, Egypt. It is a city of temples built over 2000 years and is dedicated to the Theben triad of *Amun*, *Mut* and *Khonsu*. This ancient complex is the work of several pharaohs and is dedicated to the supreme deity Amon-Ra. The site is full of several huge temples, columns, pylons and obelisks. The Karnak Temple complex was listed as a World Heritage Site by UNESCO in 1998.

24 Kimberly Diamond Mine

Kimberley in South Africa is home to the world's largest diamond mine. It is also known as the 'Big Hole'. This hole is so large that it is visible from space!

At Kimberley, the visitors can see a short film about the location and the history of diamond mining in Africa. They can also walk on a high platform to see The Big Hole, take a ride down a faux mining shaft, enter a locked vault to see real diamonds of all colours, and also visit a small museum.

25 Lalibela

The small mountain village of **Lalibela** is known for its collection of 11 medieval churches. There is a legend which says that a visit to Jerusalem in the 13th century inspired King Lalibela to rebuild the holy city in Ethiopia. Workers were engaged to carve these churches out of the area's red volcanic rock. A remarkable group of four churches was created from the same massive piece and afterwards were connected by underground passageways. Those churches were The House of Emmanuel, House of Mercurios, House of Gabriel and House of Abba Libanos.

26 Light House of Alexandria

The **Lighthouse of Alexandria** was the seventh wonder of the ancient world. It stood on the island of Pharos in Alexandria, Egypt. The entire structure was about 122 m tall including the base. It was as tall as a 40-storey skyscraper, and had giant statues of gods watching over the seafarers. Ptolemy I Soter, commander of Alexandria, in Egypt, ordered the construction of this building. It took 12 years to build. This tall tower was destroyed in an earthquake in the 1300s. The light on the top of the lighthouse was visible from 35 miles. Socrates, the Greek scholar is thought to have been the architect.

27 Marrakesh

Marrakesh is an imperial, fascinating city situated at the foot of the Atlas Mountains in Morocco. It is full of history, culture and is beautiful. It was founded in 1062 by Sultan Youssef ben Tachfine who is said to have built the defensive walls that encircle the city. The wall varies in colour between pink and red with 200 square towers (*borjs*) and nine huge gates. Marrakesh is heavily packed with labyrinthine alleyways, snake charmers, donkey carts, trendy and silver leather wares.

28 Pyramids of Giza

The **Great Pyramids of Giza** in Egypt was listed as one of the 7 wonders of the ancient world. These huge stone structures were built around 4500 years ago! In about 2,550 B.C. Pharaoh Khufu ordered the construction of his tomb on the plateau of Giza which lies on the outskirts of Cairo. The Pyramid of Khufu is also known as the Great Pyramid. Three smaller pyramids lie right by the Great Pyramid of Giza. They are the Great Pyramid of Khufu, the Great Pyramid of Khafre and the Great Pyramid of Menkaure. The Pyramids of Giza were collectively designated a World Heritage Site in 1979.

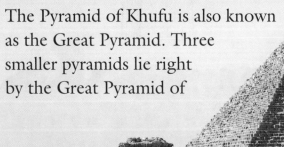

29 Suez Canal

The **Suez Canal**, located in Egypt, is a 163 km long canal that connects the Mediterranean Sea with the Red Sea. It was opened in November 1869 but has undergone many updates and expansions. The Suez Canal was important because it shortened the distance for trade routes between Europe and the Middle East and Asia.

30 Timbuktu

Timbuktu, is a city in Mali near the River Niger. Timbuktu was founded in the 11th century by the Tuareg barbers of Sahara as a seasonal camp. By the 14th century when it was part of the Mali Empire, it had become one of the major commercial centres of the West Sudan region, well-known for its gold trade. The city was designated a UNESCO World Heritage Site in 1988.

31 Valley of Kings

In the ancient times, Egyptians built massive public monuments to bury their pharaohs. They also spent a lot of time and money creating hidden underground mausoleums that no one was supposed to see. The **Valley of the Kings** which lie on the Nile's west bank near Luxor, is a valley which is full of such mausoleums. During the period 1539-1075 B.C., the valley became a royal burial ground for pharaohs such as Tutankhamen, Seti I, and Ramses II. Queens, high priests, and others also were buried here.

The Valley of Kings has two main branches— the East Valley and the West valley. It is the East Valley where most of the royal tombs are situated.

32 Antarctica

Antarctica is the icy continent at the South Pole of our planet. It is covered by permafrost (permanently frozen ground). Antarctica has the world's largest desert. 98% of the land is covered by ice sheets and the remaining 2% of land is barren rock. Antarctica has about 87% of the world's ice!

As the South Pole is the coldest, windiest, and driest place on Earth, so is Antarctica.

The coldest temperature ever recorded here was -128.6°F or -88.0°C!

There are no permanent human residents due to the extreme weather; although scientific expeditions visit Antarctica. There are about 4,000 seasonal visitors to Antarctica.

33 Deception Island

One of the most incredible islands on the planet is the **Deception Island**. It is ring-shaped and one of Antarctica's most well-known volcanoes, containing a 7-km-wide caldera flooded by the sea. It was formed by a volcanic crater, and when part of the crater collapsed, seawater rushed into the caldera and created one of the largest natural harbours in the world.

The Deception Island consists of barren volcanic slopes, steaming beaches and ash-layered glaciers. Scientists, geologists,

environmentalists and volcanologists come to study the natural phenomena. But countless tourists come to swim in the Antarctic, at Pendulum Cove in the water heated by an active volcano! This is the hot tub of Deception Island.

34 Ice Towers of Mount Erebus

Mount Erebus is one of the largest active volcanoes on Earth. It is also the only place in the world where fire and ice combine! This combination of fire and ice culminates into the birth of an ice tower height of which is about 20 m. Hot air from the volcano blows through the mouth of the ice tower. The landscape here looks spectacular. Hundreds of ice towers are stuck on Mount Erebus. It is only in this active volcano that hot lava meets cold ice creating something unique.

35 Ross Ice Shelf

Ice shelves are thick plates of ice, formed continuously by glaciers, which float on the surface of an ocean. These ice shelves act as 'brakes' for the glaciers preventing them from moving too fast into the ocean.

The **Ross Ice Shelf** is one of many such shelves. It is the largest body of floating ice in the world with an area of roughly 487, 000 square km, about the size of France! It is several hundred metres thick. In some places, the ice shelf is almost 750 m thick. The ice shelf was named after Captain James Clark Ross who discovered it on January 28, 1841.

36 Baishui Terrace

Baishui Terrace is located at the foot of Haba Snow Mountain, 103 km away from Shangri-la in China. It rises 2,380 m above the sea level. Baishui Terrace is a marvellous geological site because it was formed as calcium carbonate dissolved in the spring. The terrace is 3 square kilometres in area. The formations of this amazing creation resemble a frozen cascading series of short waterfalls.

The terraces gradually formed over many hundreds of years when running spring water rich in bicarbonate calcium left behind the calcium sediment that built the terrace walls and basins bit by bit.

37 Bali

The beautiful island of **Bali** is in Southeast Asia. It is blessed with a remarkably beautiful nature. Endless sand beaches envelope most of Bali's shores, where silvery waves come and go. Tall cliffs border the eastern shores. Volcanic mountains crown the centre of Bali. Green forests stretch on the northern part of Bali. The beaches of Bali are magnificent! There are four lakes in Bali. Lake Batur, the old crater of Mount Batur, is the largest. The 'Bali Barat National Park' in Bali is the place where it has all its forests. The forests are all dedicated to the preservation of wildlife.

38 Banaue Rice Terraces

The **Banaue Rice Terraces** of Philippines have been said to be the 8th wonder of the world. They were carved from the hillside by the tribe people of Ifugao about 2,000-3,000 years ago. They did this with their bare hands and crude implements, without using machinery to level the steps. The most wondrous fact remains that the rice terraces are still used today!

This is considered to be one of the greatest engineering feats of mankind, because if each one were connected end to end, then they would reach halfway across the globe! In 1995, the Banaue Rice Terraces were declared a World Heritage Site by UNESCO.

39 Cappadocia

Cappadocia is an area generally regarded as the plains and the mountainous region of eastern central Anatolia around the River Kizilirmak (Red River) in Turkey. It was the land of the Hittites in the ancient times. The scantily inhabited landscape of Cappadocia is full of red sandstone and salt deposits of the Tertiary period. This southern part of Cappadocia, the more densely populated, is often spoken of as the heart of the region. Cappadocia is best known for potatoes, fruits and wine.

40 Chocolate Hills

The **Chocolate Hills** are strangely coloured hills in the region of Bohol, Philippines. There are about 1,776 hills covered with grass spread over an area of more than 50 square kilometres. During the dry season, the rainfall is so inadequate that the grass dries up and turns chocolate brown giving the hills their colour and the name. The Chocolate Hills are a famous tourist attraction of Bohol. They are featured in the flag of Bohol and the seal.

41 Dead Sea

The **Dead Sea** is actually a salt lake lying on the borders of Jordan in the east, and Israel in the west! It is the lowest elevation on the surface of the Earth. Its surface and shores are 422 m below sea level! It is also one of the world's saltiest bodies of water. Due to the presence of high quantities of salt animals don't survive here. Hence the name. It is 67 km long and 18 km wide at its widest point. Anyone can easily float in the Dead Sea because of natural buoyancy.

Its water contains more than 35 different types of minerals that are essential for the health and care of the body and the skin. They are well-known for relieving pains and sufferings caused by arthritis, rheumatism, psoriasis, eczema, headache and foot-ache, while nourishing and softening the skin.

42 Guilin Hills

Guilin, is a beautiful city lying in the Northeast Guangxi Zhuang in South China. Situated on the west bank of the Li River, Guilin means 'forest of osmanthus' in Chinese. The city of Guilin in China, is well-known for the limestone hills that form the unique landscape, making it one of the most incredibly beautiful places in China. Visitors from all over the world marvel and wonder how Nature has created such a wonderful land.

Guilin is rich with rivers, and the water is limpid like mirrors reflecting the beautiful hills. The Li River passing through the region is the centre of Guilin's natural beauty.

43 Halong Bay

The **Halong Bay** is located in Quáng Ninh province, Vietnam. The bay consists of thousands of limestone karsts and isles of many different sizes and shapes. The coastline of this bay is 120 km. Many of the islands are hollow with enormous caves. The shallow waters consist of 200 species of fish and 450 different kinds of mollusks. Halong Bay is again full of lakes inside the limestone islands.

44 Jeju Island Lava Tubes

Jeju Island is a volcanic island in Korea. It is 130 km off the southern coast of South Korea. It has a lot to offer—mountains, striking coastal rock formations and the rarest system of cave lava tubes in the world with its multi-coloured carbonate roofs and floors, and dark-coloured lava walls. It's on the UNESCO World Heritage Site list.

The Jeju caves have towers of hardened lava, while the Cheju-do cliffs have tube-like formations quite similar to the Giant's Causeway in Northern Ireland.

45 Jiuzhaigou National Park

Jiuzhaigou Valley is a national park and nature reserve located in northern Sichuan province of southwestern China. It is a part of the Min Mountains on the edge of the Tibetan Plateau and stretches over 728.43km².

Jiuzhaigou Valley is known for its many multi-level waterfalls, colourful lakes, and snow-capped peaks. This valley contains a network of connected lakes, waterfalls and rivers the most spectacular of which are the Pearl Waterfalls.

Jiuzhaigou Valley was included in the list of UNESCO as a World Heritage Site in 1992.

46 Ladakh

Ladakh, in other words, 'land of high passes' is the land of many passes, snow clad mountains and arid land. It is among the highest of the world's inhabited plateaus. The summer temperatures exceed up to 35 °C, whereas in winter they may drop to -40 °C in some high altitude areas. Ladakh has been described as the 'Moon Land', 'Magic Land', and 'Mysterious Land' for its unique landscape and exquisite culture.

The location of Ladakh is quite extraordinary. It is sandwiched between two long mountain systems, the Karakoram in the north and the Himalaya in the south.

The people of Ladakh are predominantly, Tibetans and Mons. The flora and fauna are of rare kind here.

47 Lake Baikal

Lake Baikal in south-east Siberia, is the deepest lake in the world. The surface area of the lake is 31470 square kilometres, when its water level is 454 m above sea level. The maximum depth of the lake is 1637 m.

It is noteworthy that Lake Baikal contains 20% of all fresh running water on the planet. This makes it the single largest reservoir of freshwater. The lake contains an extraordinary variety of flora and fauna, of exceptional value to evolutionary science. It is often referred to as the 'Galápagos of Russia'.

48 Mayon Volcano

Mayon Volcano, the most famous of the active volcanoes of the Philippines is the world's most perfect cone. It is said to be a perfect stratovolcano rising to 2462 m on Luzon Island dominating the city of Legaspi. This well-known volcano has a base 130 km in circumference and rises to 2,462 m from the shores of Albay Gulf. This is very popular with climbers and campers. It is the centre of Mayon Volcano National Park. Since 1616, there have been more than 30 eruptions. Mayon has a symmetrical cone. Like other volcanoes in the Pacific Ocean, Mayon is a part of the 'Pacific Ring of Fire'.

49 Mt. Bromo

Mt. Bromo is actually a small active volcano inside the much larger caldera of an ancient extinct volcano. It is in East Java and one of Indonesia's most scenic destinations. The name of Bromo has been derived from Javanese pronunciation of Brahma, the Hindu creator God. While the volcano is still active and has recently been closed off for public, it's still a point of pilgrimage for Javanese Hindus.

50 Mt. Everest

Mount Everest is the world's highest mountain above sea level at 8,848 m. It is located in the Himalayan Range of mountains on Nepal-Tibet border. Everest was named after an ex-British Surveyor General of India, Sir George Everest.

The Himalayas was formed about 60 million years ago when the Indian sub-continent collided with Asia. However, the Himalayas are still growing. They grow approximately 2.4 inches higher every year! It is interesting to note that until 1852 Everest was not considered the highest mountain on earth. It was only in 1852 when Radhanath Sikdar, an Indian mathematician and surveyor from Bengal, first identified Everest as the world's highest peak. The first persons to climb the mountain successfully were Edmund Hillary and Tenzing Norgay in 1953.

51 Mt. Fuji

Mount Fuji is the highest volcano and highest peak in Japan. Fuji is a perfect stratovolcano which lies to the south-west of Tokyo. This unique volcanic mountain with an exceptionally symmetrical shape has become the icon of Japanese art. It is a popular destination for excursions. More than 200,000 people climb to the top of the Mt Fuji every year. Mt Fuji had its last eruption in the year 1707–08.

Mount Fuji is a symbol of Japan. It is probably the most popular tourist site in Japan. It has been observed that more than 200,000 people climb to the summit every year, mostly during the summer months.

52 Mt. Taishan

Mount Taishan, has been held in high esteem by the Chinese people since ages. Its main peak rises 1,545 m above sea level. Mt. Taishan is located at Taishan City of Shandong Province, China. Since ancient times, it is known as the 'First of the Five Sacred Mountains', and it is situated on the Central Plains of the country. The reputation of this peak comes mostly from its cultural significance. It was considered to be a sacred place by the Emperors of the Zhou Dynasty.

53 Mud Volcanoes

The term mud volcano or mud dome refers to formations created by geo-excreted liquids and gases. Most of the mud volcanoes are found in Gobustan, Azerbaijan and the Caspian Sea. In Azerbaijan, eruptions happen from a deep mud reservoir which is connected to the surface even during dormant periods. In 2001, one mud volcano situated 15 km from Baku made world headlines when it suddenly started spewing flames 15 m high!

The mud is thought to have medicinal qualities.

54 Pangong Tso Lake

The **Pangong Tso Lake** is a saltwater lake deep in the Himalayas at an altitude of 4,350 m. It lies across a disputed border area between India and China-governed Tibet. It is situated in the barren lands of Ladakh. It is the one of biggest lakes in Asia. Interestingly, one third of it is in India and remaining in China. It is 130 km long and 7 km wide. This lake is located on the Changtang plateau, and is also known as hollow lake. The brackish water of the lake plays with sun light to produce different effect with colour, surrounded by tall mountains.

55 Puerto Princesa

The City of **Puerto Princesa** is located in the southwest of Manila in Philippines. It is famous for the longest crossable and the most beautiful underground river in the world. It is 8.2 km in length and it moves through a beautiful cave before emptying into the South China Sea.

The river flows directly into the sea, and the lower portion of the river is subject to tidal influences. According to folk legend the name 'Puerto Princesa' comes from a princess-like woman who is said to have roamed around the place on certain nights of the year.

56 Reed Flute Cave

The **Reed Flute Cave** is a landmark and tourist attraction in Guilin, Guangxi, China. It is a natural limestone cave which is over 180 million years old. The cave got its name from the type of reed growing outside, which can be made into melodious flutes. A large number of stalactites, stalagmites and rock formations in strange shapes fill the caves. Inside the cave, there are more than 70 inscriptions written in ink, which dates back to as far as 792 AD.

57 Ring of Fire

The **Pacific Ring of Fire**, or just **Ring of Fire** is a basin in the Pacific Ocean, an area where a large number of earthquakes and volcanic eruptions occur. This area is like an arc stretching from New Zealand, along the eastern edge of Asia, north across the Aleutian Islands of Alaska, and south along the coast of North and South America.

The area is in the horseshoe shape, and is associated with a continuous series of oceanic trenches, volcanic arcs and volcanic belts.

The Ring of Fire has 452 volcanoes and is home to over 75% of the world's active and dormant volcanoes.

58 Taal Volcano

The **Taal Volcano** is located in the island of Philippines. This volcano is a part of a chain of volcanoes along the western side of the island of Luzon. This tiny volcano is said to be smallest active volcano in the world and is about 700 m high. The volcano has erupted violently and severely many times. Till now, around 6000 people have lost their lives because of its eruptions!

59 The Shilin Stone Forest

The **Shilin Stone Forest** is spread over 350 square kilometres in Yunnan province of China. These stone needles look like a forest. The rock formations stand tall and emerge vertically from the ground. These karst rocks are more than 270 million years old! The local people believe in a legend which says the forest was created when a young woman was forbidden to marry her love. She is said to have rebelled by turning herself into stone.

60 Ajanta Caves

The rock cut caves of **Ajanta** are situated in India. They are about 107 km from the Aurangabad city in the state of Maharashtra. The 29 rock-cut caves of Ajanta exist in the shape of a massive horse shoe. The caves exhibit some of the finest examples of early Buddhist architecture. They include caves-paintings and sculptures dedicated to Lord Buddha. The caves have been included in the UNESCO World Heritage Site since 1983.

61 Akashi Kaikyo Bridge

Akashi Kaikyo Bridge, also known as the 'Pearl Bridge' is located in Japan and considered as Japan's finest example of commendable engineering skills. Akashi Kaiko Bridge is said to be the world's longest suspension bridge with a length of 3911 m. It serves as a link between the city of Kobe and Iwaya by crossing the Akashi strait. This remarkable bridge took 12 years to get completed. The Akashi Kaikyo Bridge has been designed to withstand earthquakes and harsh sea conditions. It took two million workers to construct the bridge, over ten years and with 181,000 tons of steel.

62 Ankor Wat

Angkor, in Cambodia's northern province is one of the most important archaeological sites of Southeast Asia. It consists of many temples, basins, dykes, reservoirs and canals. Angkor Archaeological Park contains the magnificent remains of the different capitals of the Khmer Empire, which existed between 9th and 15th century. Temples such as *Angkor Wat, the Bayon, Preah Khan and Ta Prohm*, are all examples of Khmer architecture. Angkor is considered to be a symbol of high architectural, archaeological and artistic significance.

63 Anuradhapura

Anuradhapura is a sacred city of Sri Lankan civilization now in picturesque ruins. This sacred city was established around a cutting from the 'tree of enlightenment'— the Buddha's fig tree. For a long time it was hidden away in dense jungle for many years in ruins. The fascinating ancient ruins include huge *bell-shaped stupas, temples, sculptures, palaces, and ancient drinking-water reservoirs.*

Anuradhapura went on to become a Ceylonese political and religious capital in the 4th century BC and flourished for 1,300 years. Today, it draws many Buddhist pilgrims and visitors from all over the world.

64 Ayutthaya

The Historic **City of Ayutthaya**, which was founded in 1350, in Thailand was the second capital of the Siamese Kingdom. Its remains which is full of gigantic monasteries, give a picture of its past glory.

Ayutthaya flourished between the 14th to the 18th centuries. During this time, it grew to be one of the world's largest and most cosmopolitan urban areas and a centre of politics and commerce. The location of Ayutthaya was very strategic. It was located on an island surrounded by three rivers connecting the city to the sea. This site was chosen because it prevented the attack of the city by the sea-going warships of other nations!

65 Baalbek

The complex of temples at **Baalbek** is located at the foot of the south-west slope of Anti-Lebanon, at an altitude of 1150 m. The huge constructions of Baalbek city built over a period of more than two centuries, make it one of the most famous Roman religious sites. Pilgrims gathered at this sanctuary to worship the three deities, known as the Romanized Triad of Heliopolis (Jupiter, Venus and Mercury).

66 Bagan Temples and Pagodas

Bagan is an ancient city located in the Mandalay Region of Myanmar. It was the capital of the Kingdom of Pagan from the 9th to 13th centuries and the city was the first kingdom to unify the regions that would later make up the modern country of Myanmar. When this kingdom was at the peak of its political power, over 10,000 Buddhist temples, pagodas and monasteries were constructed in the Bagan plains alone. Among these remains, of over 2200 temples and pagodas still survive to the present day. The golden Shwezigon Paya is one of its most important religious buildings.

67 Bara Imambara

The **Bara Imambara** is a complex in the city of Lucknow, India. It was built in the year 1784 by the fourth Nawab of Awadh, Asaf-ud-Daula. It is an important place of worship for the Muslims.

The Bara Imambara has a unique style of construction. The central hall of Bara Imambara is the largest arched hall in the world! Blocks have been put together with interlocking system of bricks. Girders and beams have not been used at all. But the roof stands steady till date without any support!

The Bara Imambara is known for its incredible maze called Bhulbhulaiya. The panorama of the city can be seen from the top of this monument.

68 Beppu

Beppu, is a relatively small city in Japan, which is famous for its unique hot springs.

This unique city is located on the island of Kyushu, between Beppu Bay and Mount Tsurumi. It contains the highest number of thermal sources in Japan second only to Yellow Stone National Park.

There are 11 types of *'onsen'* (in Japanese) or hot springs globally and 10 of these types are available in Beppu! Beppu has an unusual 670 hot springs in total, spread over 8 major thermal districts called 'Beppu Hatto'.

69 Borobodur

Borobudur is in Java, Indonesia. The name Borobudur means 'many Buddhas'. It is one of the greatest Buddhist monuments in the world. It was built in the 8th and 9th centuries AD during the reign of the Syailendra Dynasty. The monument has 1500 panels carved with scenes of the Buddha's life. More than 500 Buddha statues are perched around the temple. The compound also comprises of a balustrade and nearly 3,000 bas-relief sculptures illustrating the life and teachings of the

Buddha. It was designated a UNESCO World Heritage Site in 1991.

70 Burj Al Arab

The **Burj Al Arab** is a luxury hotel in Dubai, United Arab Emirates. The word Burj Al Arab means '*The Arabian Tower*' in Arabic. This luxury hotel offers some of the highest levels of personalized services one can imagine! This super luxury hotel stands tall at 321 m on an artificial island. It is the fourth tallest hotel in the world resembling the sail of a boat. Burj Al Arab was designed by Tom Wright and was completed in 1999. It houses 202 rooms, 18 elevators and 60 floors. Each suite has its own private butler!

71 Burj Khalifa

The **Burj Khalifa** is a skyscraper in the amazing city of Dubai. It is the tallest building in the world. It is 828 m into the sky. This unique tall-rise building has 162 floors. One may get a 360° view of the city from the 124th floor. The construction of Burj Khalifa began in 2004. The expenditure of building it exceeded $20 billion. Nearly 12,000 people worked on it. The Burj Khalifa has the highest mosque (158th floor) and the highest swimming pool (76th floor) in the world. The official opening of the building in 2010 was adorned with fireworks and colourful celebrations.

72 Chengde Mountain Resort

The **Chengde Mountain Resort** in Hebei Province is an unusually beautiful summer resort in Beijing. Many of the Chinese Emperors spent several months of a year here to escape the summer heat. The resort consists of two parts— a court in front, where the Emperors received high officials and foreign envoys and bedchambers at the rear end. This beautiful resort was listed as the World Heritage by UNESCO in 1994.

73 Church of the Holy Sepulchre

Jerusalem's **Church of the Holy Sepulchre** is the *holiest Christian site* in the world. Constantine, the Great was the first Roman Emperor to adopt Christianity. He made it the official religion of the Roman Empire. In Jerusalem, Queen Helena, Emperor Constantine's mother identified the place of crucifixion (the rock held to be Golgotha) and the nearby tomb known as Anastasis (Greek for resurrection). The Emperor decided to build an appropriate shrine on the site. And so, the church was built.

74 Damascus

Damascus, the capital of Syria is one of the most ancient cities in the world. The major population of the city are Muslims; Christians and Jews form the rest. It has been called the 'Pearl of the East'. There are about 125 monuments from different periods of its history. The most impressive and the most acclaimed building is the Great Mosque of the Umayyads built in the 8th century. The Old City was listed as a UNESCO Word Heritage Site in 1979.

75 Dazu Rock Carvings

The **Dazu Rock Carvings** are a series of Chinese religious sculptures and carvings. They date back to the 7th century AD. The Dazu Rock Carvings are made up of 75 well protected sites containing some 50,000 statues!

The carvings are remarkable for their aesthetic quality, and their diversity of subject matter, both secular and religious. They provide outstanding evidence of the harmonious synthesis of Buddhism, Taoism and Confucianism.

76 Dome of the Rock

The most important Islamic site in Jerusalem is the **Dome of the Rock**. An impressivse and magnificent monument, the Dome of the Rock can be seen from all over Jerusalem. Like the Ka'ba in Mecca, it is built over a *sacred rock*. But the Dome of the Rock is not a mosque, but an Islamic shrine. It is believed that this was the place from which Prophet Muhammad ascended into heaven. The historical monument was built by the Umayyad Caliph Abd al-Malik from 688 to 691 AD.

On the other hand, Jews believe that the rock is the very place where Abraham prepared to sacrifice Isaac.

77 Ellora Caves

The caves of **Ellora** are an impressive complex of Buddhist, Hindu and Jain temples near the ancient Indian village of Ellora, near Aurangabad in India. There are 34 caves in all. Among them, there are 12 Buddhist caves, 17 Hindu caves and 5 Jain caves. It has been observed that the Hindu caves are the most spectacular in design. The most extraordinary of the cave temples is Kailasa which is cave number 16. The Ellora caves were included by UNESCO as a World Heritage Site in 1983.

78 Ephesus

Ephesus was an ancient Greek city well-known for the 'Temple of Artemis'. It was one of the seven wonders of the ancient world. This city was second in size to Rome. Emperor Constantine I rebuilt much of the city and also got new public baths constructed. Ephesus is also famous for having the house where Mother Mary lived! The 'Library of Celsius', is perhaps one of the most photographed buildings among the ruins of Ephesus. This ancient city also contains a theater, the Temple of Artemis, the Basilica of St. John, the Temple of Domitian and the Temple of Hadrian among other ancient monuments.

79 Forbidden City

The **Forbidden City** also called Palace Museum, is a remarkable palace situated in the Tiananmen Square in Beijing, China. It was the royal palace for twenty-four emperors during the Ming and Qing dynasties. It took 14 long years to build it. The Forbidden Palace is rectangular in shape and is the world's largest palace complex. It is surrounded by a 52 m wide moat and a 10 m high wall and has more than 8,700 rooms! The Forbidden City was declared a World Heritage Site in 1987 and is listed by UNESCO as the largest collection of ancient wooden structures in the world which has been preserved.

80 Golden Temple

The Harmandir Sahib or Hari Mandir is a gurudwara in India (Amritsar) in the state of Punjab which is the holiest shrine in Sikhism. It is popularly known as the Golden Temple. The temple (or *gurdwara*) is a major pilgrimage destination for Sikhs from all over the world.

The construction of the Golden Temple began in the year 1574. It was constructed on a piece of land donated by the Mughal Emperor, Akbar. The gurudwara was completed in 1601, but restoration and its decoration continued for many years. Later, 100 kg of gold were applied to the inverted lotus-shaped dome and decorative marble was added to it later in the early 19th century. All this embellishment work took place under the patronage of Maharaja Ranjit Singh.

81 Gomateswara

The **Gomateshwara** statue depicts Lord Gomateshwara, a Jain saint. It is in Sravanabelagola, in the state of Karnataka, India. The statue is 17 m high and stands majestically on top of a hill. The Gomateshwara Statue was build out of a single large stone. It is the tallest monolithic statue in the world. Every 12 years, the Jain devotees celebrate the Mahamastakabhisheka festival. During the festival, the statue of Lord Gomateswara is bathed with milk, curds, ghee, saffron and gold coins.

82 Great Buddha of Kamakura

The **Great Buddha of Kamakura** is an outdoor bronze statue of Amida Buddha. It is located in the city of Kamakura, Japan. This massive statue is seated serenely in the grounds of *Kotokuin* and forms one of the icons of Japan. It is 13.35 m high and weighs approximately 93000 kg. The Great Buddha is seated in the lotus position with his hands forming the *Dhyani Mudra* or the gesture of meditation. In the beautiful backdrop of the hills, the great statue of Buddha is a truly marvellous sight.

83 Great Wall of China

The **Great Wall of China** is one of the largest architectural pieces to have ever been completed! It was built over 2000 years ago by Qin Shihuangdi, the first Emperor of China. It was made to prevent the raids by the nomadic people who tried to enter China. It is the longest wall of the world. The wall is a simple structure built of mud, stone and brick. It is one of the wonders of the world and also a UNESCO World Heritage Site.

84 Hagia Sophia

The Byzantine Church of **Hagia Sophia** stands on the top of the first hill of Constantinople in modern Istanbul. The ancient church was built by Justinian I between 532 and 537. It is also called the 'Church of the Holy Wisdom'. The Hagia Sophia was first a church, then a mosque and now a museum. It is one of the greatest surviving examples of Byzantine architecture, richly adorned with mosaics and marble pillars.

85 Hampi

The grand site of **Hampi** was the last capital of the last great Hindu Kingdom of Vijayanagar. Hampi is a village located in the state of Karnataka in India. Besides the beautiful temples, there is an impressive complex of royal and public buildings like elephant stables, Queen's Bath, Lotus Mahal, bazaars and markets. There are more than 500 monuments here. In 1986, it was designated a UNESCO World Heritage Site.

86 Hanging Garden of Babylon

The **Hanging Gardens of Babylon** were built by Nebuchadnezzar II about 2,500 years ago. He made this beautiful garden to make his wife Amytis happy because she didn't like the Babylonian desert. She hailed from Persia, which had many plants and fountains.

The Hanging Gardens were known to be in Mesopotamia, near present day Baghdad in Iraq. This historical garden was located by the Euphrates River. It was about 106.68m tall and was covered with trees, flowers, lawns, plants, fountains, pools, and also miniature water falls! The garden had every kind of plant available in the kingdom and was made of mud brick and stone. It had a series of terraces, one on top of the other. The plants couldn't survive without water. So, water from the Euphrates River had to be pumped to flow through channels to the plants.

87 Hanging Monastry

The Hengshan **Hanging Monastery** stands at the foot of Mt Hengshan, near Datong City in China. Since the monasteries cling to the cliff and seem to be hanging, they are called the 'Hanging Monastries'. These unique monasteries hang on the west cliff of Jinxia Gorge more than 50 m above the ground! It was built in AD 491. The pavilions are mostly built of wood. The monks have also expanded the pavilions by digging caves in the cliff behind them. These caves contain religious statues as well as the statue of Buddha, Confucius and Laotsu sitting side by side.

88 Hermitage Museum

The **Hermitage Museum** in Russia is one of the most well-known museums of the world. It is huge and spread over several buildings. It is St. Petersburg's most popular tourist attractions. With over 3 million items in its collection, the visitors get to see a wide variety of objects from Impressionist masterpieces to fascinating treasures from the Orient.

The Hermitage was once the palace of Catherine the Great, who used it as a private place of solitude. The rooms on the first floor are breathtaking, as they still retain the look of the Imperial times. The second floor is not that remarkable but has many important French paintings.

89 Hirano Shrine

The **Hirano Shrine** which is located in the northwest of Kyoto was established in the year 794. This shrine is well-known for its gardens and trees. From the very earliest years of its inception, the shrine has shared a strong relationship with the imperial family. The shrine has been the venue of an annual cherry blossom festival since long. The cherry blossom festival has become the oldest regularly held festival in Kyoto.

90 Isfahan

The large province of **Isfahan** is located at the centre of Iran. This province was largely the work of Shah Abbas I, commonly known as 'Shah Abbas the Great'. He made Isfahan his capital city in 1598 and rebuilt it with magnificent parks and gorgeous avenues. He surrounded the grand Naqsh-e Jahan Square with four monumental structures— the mosaic-tiled Royal Mosque, the Portico of Qaysariyyeh, the Mosque of Sheykh Lotfollah and the royal gardens to the west. Naqsh-e Jahan Square was constructed in order to hold markets, celebrate festivals and games of polo.

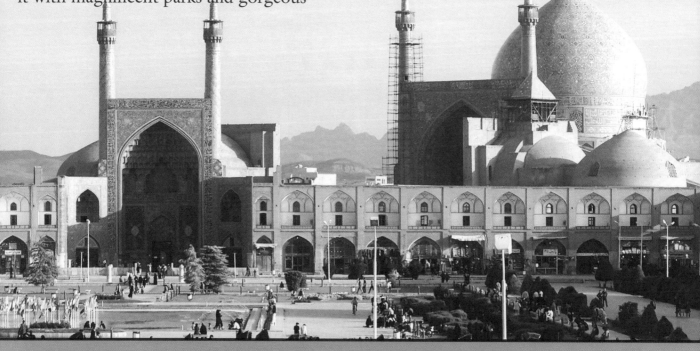

91 Itsukushima Shrine

Itsukushima, also known as Miyajima, is a sacred island about 20 km southwest of Hiroshima city. Miyajima, which literally means 'shrine-island' in Japanese, refers to the island which has risen to fame due to the, Itsukushima Shrine. The shrine complex, consists of many acclaimed National Treasures of Japan. These national treasures were included in the UNESCO World Heritage Site in 1996 for its religious, architectural and artistic importance.

The shrine is built in a small cove. It stands on a pier-like structure and at full tide it seems to be floating on the water!

92 Jaisalmer

Jaisalmer is one of the major tourist attractions in the state of Rajasthan, India. It is the centre for performing arts and well-known for its craft and paintings. The history of Jaisalmer can be traced back to 1156 A.D., when Rawal Jaisal established his kingdom in the middle of the huge, arid Thar Desert. This historical city is well-known for its cobbled streets, beautiful palaces, forts, temples and havelis (mansions). Nearly all the houses here, are exquisitely carved, having filigreed work all over. The main attraction of this exquisite city is the magnificent Jaisalmer fort. The city is popularly known as the 'golden city' as most of the houses are made of sand stone which is golden yellow in colour.

93 Jantar Mantar

Jantar Mantar is situated in the modern city of Delhi, India. It was built by Maharaja Jai Singh II of Jaipur in 1724. It is an astronomical observation site. It consists of 13 architectural astronomy instruments. The etymological meaning of Jantar Mantar is 'instrument for calculation'. The main purpose of Jantar Mantar was to assemble astronomical tables and foretell the times and movements of the heavenly bodies of sun, moon and planets. There are four distinct parts of Jantar Mantar— the Samrat, Ram, Jayaprakash, and Mishra Yantras.

94 Jerusalem Old City

Jerusalem has always had a significant position as a holy city for the religions of Judaism, Christianity and Islam. It is prominent for the Muslims because it is the site from where the Prophet Muhammad departed to heaven; for the Jews because it is the home of the Wailing Wall (remains of the Second Temple); and finally for the Christians because it is the place where Jesus Christ was crucified.

This ancient city houses 220 historic monuments among which the Dome of Rock stands out.

95 Jiayuguan Fort

The **Jiayuguan Fort** is located near the Jiayuguan City of Gansu Province of China. The Jiayuguan Fort dates back to the Ming Dynasty, and to this day stands as a symbol of a rich history. Due to its strategic geographical location and imposing architectures, Jiayuguan Fort is considered to be unconquerable.

96 Kampong Thom Province

Kampong Thom Province is Cambodia's oldest temple complex built during the 7th century. This complex consisting of 52 standing temples of Sambor Prei Kuk are part of the remains of the former capital of Chenla, an ancient kingdom that once ruled much of present-day Cambodia. It is believed that Kampong Thom Province is even older than the oldest temples of Angkor Vat by some 600 years! But amazingly, not many people visit the site; a meagre 5,000 annual visitors come to visit compared to the million-plus tourists who visit Angkor Wat.

97 Khajuraho

Khajuraho is a famous archaeological site in central India in the state of Madhya Pradesh. It is globally known for its sculptured temples dedicated to Lord Shiva, Lord Vishnu and Jain founders. It is listed in the UNESCO World Heritage site list. Khajuraho was one of the capitals of the Chandela kings, who ruled from the 9th to the 11th century. This magnificent site originally had about 85 temples built by different rulers; only 20 exist today. Majority of the temples were built of sandstone with varying shades.

98 Kiyomizu Temple

The **Kiyomizu Temple** or Otowa-san Kiyomizu-dera in eastern Kyoto is a temple dedicated to the Hoss school of Buddhism. The most remarkable aspect about this temple is that not a single nail is used to building it! The temple has a main hall with a huge veranda that is supported by pillars and juts out over the hillside. Just below this hall, is the waterfall Otowa-no-taki, the water of which is therapeutic. The Kiyomizu temple complex also consists of some other shrines like the Jishu shrine built in honour of the God of love, Okuninushi.

99 Leshan Great Buddha

Leshan Giant Buddha is the largest Buddha statue in the world. It draws millions of tourists and Buddhist pilgrims from all over the world. This Giant Buddha lies to the east of the city of Leshan in Sichuan Province in China. The statue faces the sacred Mount Emei with rivers flowing below its feet.

The Leshan Buddha statue is a stout, smiling monk, calmly sitting resting his hands upon his knees.

The statue has a remarkable size. It stands 70 m tall. Its head is 15 m high, while its nose is 6 m long and its fingers are 3 m long each!

100 Li River Cruise

Li River is one of China's most famous scenic areas. It is the largest and the most beautiful scenic areas in China and attracts thousands of visitors each year. The Li River flows its way southeast for about 437 km, passing through Guilin, Yangshuo, Pingle, Zhaoping and finally meets Xi River in Wulin. This unusual landscape is decorated with rolling hills, steep cliffs, mysterious caves and leisurely boats. The 83 km river trip takes four to five hours and never disappoints us.

101 Massada

Masada is a mountainous natural fortress in the Judaean Desert overlooking the Dead Sea. It was built by Herod the Great, King of Judaea as a palace complex, in the classic Roman style.

Massada's archaeological site holds great significance. When Judaea became a province of the Roman Empire, Massada became the shelter of the last survivors of the Jewish revolt, who chose death rather than slavery when the Romans conquered. Massada has great emblematic value for the Jewish people.

102 Mausoleum of Halicarnassus

The **Mausoleum at Halicarnassus** was a tomb at Halicarnassus in present Turkey. It was built for Mausolus the ruler of Halicarnassus by Queen Artemisia II, who was both his wife and his sister. The Mausoleum of Halicarnassus was one of the ancient Seven Wonders of the World. It was shining white and the burial chamber was decorated with gold. The roof of this beautiful structure had a sculpture of four horses pulling a chariot carrying king Mausolus and his Queen Artemisia.

103 Mecca

Mecca is the holiest city of the religion of Islam. It is located in the Kingdom of Saudi Arabia. Its main importance as a holy city for Muslims lies in the fact that it was the birthplace of the founder of Islam, Prophet Mohammed.

Every year, during the Islamic month of *Dhu'l-Hijja*, countless Muslims from around the world join in a pilgrimage (*Haj*) to Mecca. The central point of Mecca is the Kaaba, the 'House of God' believed by Muslims to have been built by Abraham and his son Ishmael.

104 Meenakshi Temple

Meenakshi Temple, one of the finest Hindu temples is situated in Madurai, in the state of Tamil Nadu, India. It is one of the best examples of the Dravidian architecture. This temple complex is devoted to Lord Shiva and his wife Goddess Parvati or Meenakshi.

The whole temple complex is surrounded by 14 gateway towers or *gopurams*, among which the southern tower is more than 52 m high. The temple is visited by 15,000 visitors a day, and collects an annual revenue of sixty million rupees.

105 Nagash-e-Rostam

Nagash-e-Rostam is an unforgettable and amazing attraction in Iran. It is an ancient necropolis or burial ground located about 12 km northwest of Persepolis, in the Pars Province of Iran. It lies a few hundred metres from Naqsh-e Rajab. This Necropolis has four crosses carved into the towering rock, serving as the tombs of the mighty King Darius the Great and his three successor kings. The Greek crosses stand mightily above a series of Sassanian rock-reliefs within Persepolis, the ancient city.

106 Persepolis

The **Persepolis** ruins lie at the foot of Kuh-i-Rahmat (Mountain of Mercy) in the plain of Marv Dasht about 650 km south of Teheran. It was founded by Darius I in 518 B.C. Persepolis existed as the capital of the Achaemenid Empire which was built on a immensely large half-artificial, half-natural terrace. The king created there a magnificent palace complex inspired by Mesopotamian architectural style. The historical importance and quality of the ruins of Persepolis make it a unique archaeological site.

107 Petra

Petra is an amazing ancient city in Jordan. It is justly considered to be one of the New Seven Wonders of the World. Petra consists of tombs, temples and other majestic buildings carved from solid sandstone cliffs. The Nabataeans, who were an Arabian tribe, sculpted the buildings of Petra from the rocky cliffs. Nabataeans were extraordinary engineers. In 1985, Petra was designated a UNESCO World Heritage Site.

108 Petronas Twin Towers

Petronas Twin Towers that are among the world's tallest buildings are a pair of skyscraper office buildings in Kuala Lumpur, Malaysia. The Twin Towers were built as the headquarters of Petronas, the national petroleum company of Malaysia. Both the towers rise to a height of 451.9 m. A skybridge connects the two towers between the 41st and 42nd storeys. The construction of the twin towers took 7 years. It was finally completed in 1998.

109 Potala Palace

The **Potala Palace** is the winter palace of Dalai Lama. It is in Lhasa in Tibet. The palace complex comprises of the White and Red Palaces at an altitude of 3,700 m in the middle of the Lhasa valley. The Potala Palace was designated as a UNESCO World Heritage Site.

110 Pudong Skyline

Pudong is a new area of Shanghai, China, located along the east side of the Huangpu River. Formerly, Pudong was an under developed agricultural area. But since the 1990s, Pudong has developed rapidly and emerged as China's commercial centre.

The Pudong Skyline is an area consisting of a cluster of modern skyscrapers having amazing designs and magnificent heights. The view of this skyline is breathtaking during daytime, even better at night. The three tallest skyscrapers of Pudong are Shanghai World Financial Centre, Oriental Pearl TV Tower and Jin Mao Tower.

111 Reclining Buddha

Wat Pho or the **Temple of the Reclining Buddha** is located behind the magnificent Temple of the Emerald Buddha. This temple is the largest temple in Bangkok and is famous for its huge and majestic reclining Buddha which measures 46 m long and is golden in colour. The Buddha's feet are 3 m long and exquisitely decorated with mother-of-pearl illustrations of the Buddha.

112 Registhan Samarkhand

Samarkand is the second-largest city in Uzbekistan. It is the capital of Samarqand Province. The city is most noted for its central position on the Silk Road between China and the West, and for being an Islamic centre for scholarly study.

The Registan was the heart of the ancient city of Samarkand. The name *Registan* means 'sandy place' in Persian. The Registan actually was a public square, where people gathered to hear royal proclamations, and a place of public executions.

113 Saviour Cathedral

The Church of the 'Transfiguration of Our Saviour' is in Russia. This monument has never been closed for worship unlike most Russian places of worship. It is crowned with 22 onion-shaped domes. The shape and size of the domes vary from tier to tier. The date of construction of this religious monument is not known with precision. But probably it is late 18th to early 20th Century.

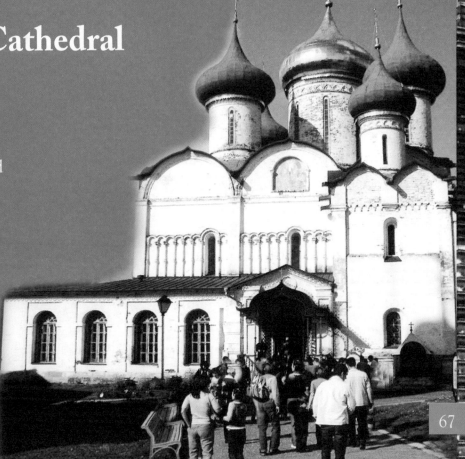

114 Shwedagon Pagoda

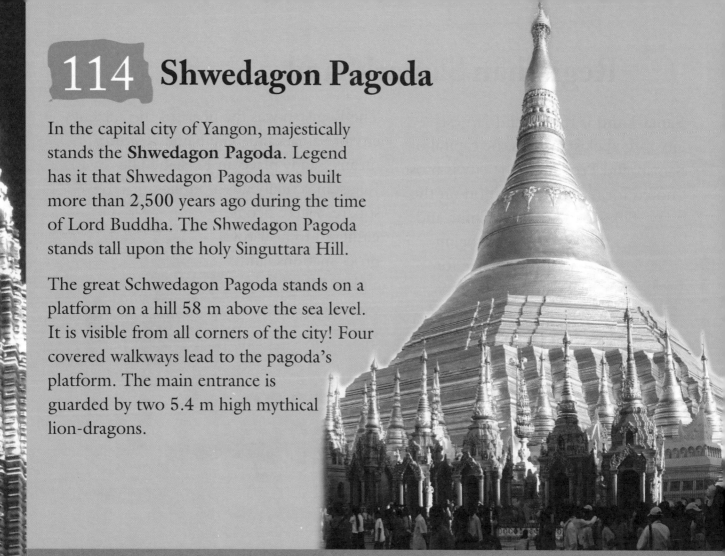

In the capital city of Yangon, majestically stands the **Shwedagon Pagoda**. Legend has it that Shwedagon Pagoda was built more than 2,500 years ago during the time of Lord Buddha. The Shwedagon Pagoda stands tall upon the holy Singuttara Hill.

The great Schwedagon Pagoda stands on a platform on a hill 58 m above the sea level. It is visible from all corners of the city! Four covered walkways lead to the pagoda's platform. The main entrance is guarded by two 5.4 m high mythical lion-dragons.

115 Sigiriya

In the north-central part of Sri Lanka lies the archeological site called **Sigiriya**. It is also known as the Lion's rock. It contains the ruins of an ancient palace complex, built during the reign of King Kasyapa who reigned between 477AD - 495 AD. The whole structure has been destroyed except for the paws of the lion that still exist. The ruins of the palace are surrounded by the ruins of an elaborate network of gardens and reservoirs. It was designated a UNESCO World Heritage Site in 1982.

116 St Basil's Cathedral

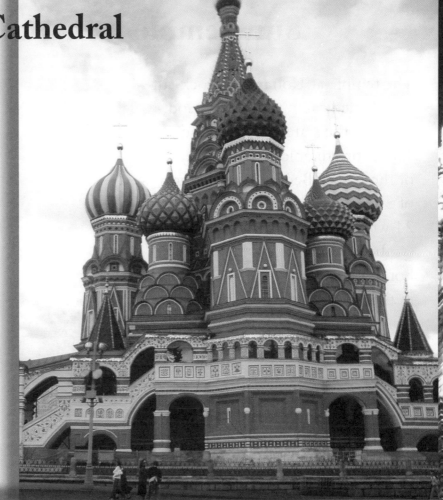

Saint Basil's Cathedral in Moscow was constructed to commemorate the victory of Ivan the Terrible over the Mongols. It is a magnificent mixture of colours and red brick towers. It combines 9 individual chapels, each with a dome. It is one of the most beautiful religious buildings in the world!

This remarkable cathedral was named St. Basil after the Saint Basil the Blessed, who was very popular in Moscow at that time.

117 Summer Palace

The **Summer Palace** in Beijing is a magnificent Chinese landscape garden design. This garden is a rare combination of natural beauty along with artificial features such as pavilions, halls, palaces, temples and bridges. It covers a large area and includes more than 3,000 buildings. It mainly consists of Kunming lake, Longevity Hill and the Long Corridor. The garden can be also divided into three parts—administration, residence and scenery browsing area.

118 Sun Temple Konark

The temple at **Konark** is a rock-cut temple dedicated to the Sun God, Surya in the state of Orissa, India. The entire temple on the shores of the Bay of Bengal is in the form of Surya's chariot. The chariot has 24 wheels and are decorated with symbolic designs. It is led by six horses. The temple was constructed in the 13th century by King Narasingh Deva. The seven horses, which pull the Sun Temple represent the days of the week. The 12 pairs of wheels represent the 12 months of the year. This temple was designated a World Heritage Site in 1984.

119 Taipei 101

Taipei 101 is a tall building located in Xinyi District, Taipei in the country of Taiwan. This landmark building comprises of 101 floors above ground and 5 floors underground.

Taipei 101 is 508 m tall and it was the 'world's tallest building' until the construction of Burj Khalifa in Dubai in 2010. The tower is designed to withstand typhoons and earthquakes. The tower contains a multi-Level shopping mall besides hundreds of fashionable stores, restaurants and clubs.

120 Taj Mahal

The **Taj Mahal** is considered to be the greatest architectural achievement in the whole range of Indo-Islamic architecture. This brilliant mausoleum of mughal architecture is situated in Agra, India on the southern bank of River Yamuna. The Taj Mahal was built by the Mughal Emperor Shah Jahan in the memory of his beloved wife Mumtaz Mahal. It took 22 years to build it. More than 20,000 men were employed. The marble out of which the Taj is made was brought from all over India and Central Asia.

To construct the Taj Mahal, masons, stone-cutters, inlayers, carvers, painters, calligraphers, dome builders and other artisans were summoned from the whole of the empire and also from Central Asia and Iran.

The Taj was included in the UNESCO World Heritage Site in 1983. It is also a part of the Seven Wonders of the World.

121 Temple of Artemis

The **Temple of Artemis**, located in Ephesus, Turkey, was built in the fourth century BC. It was built to worship the Moon Goddess, Artemis. In the middle of the temple stood a beautiful statue of Artemis which was made of marble and decorated with ivory and gold. It is said that hundreds of people came to the temple every year to see it. Visitors included merchants, common people, artisans, and kings.

122 Temple of Emerald Buddha

The **Temple of Emerald Buddha** or Wat Phar Kaew is located at Bangkok. It is the most important place of pilgrimage in Thailand. The statue of Emerald Buddha is about 0.61m tall and is made of green jasper and covered with gold. The Emerald Buddha is dressed in a seasonal costume, which is changed three times a year according to the seasons.

123 Temple of Heaven

The **Temple of Heaven** is a complex of fine cult buildings in Beijing founded in the first half of the 15th century. It is set amidst gardens. This fine temple complex covers 2,700,000 square metres. The Emperors of the Ming and Qing Dynasties used these temples for sacrificial ceremonies and for prayers. The most renowned of all the buildings is the House of Prayer for Good Harvest.

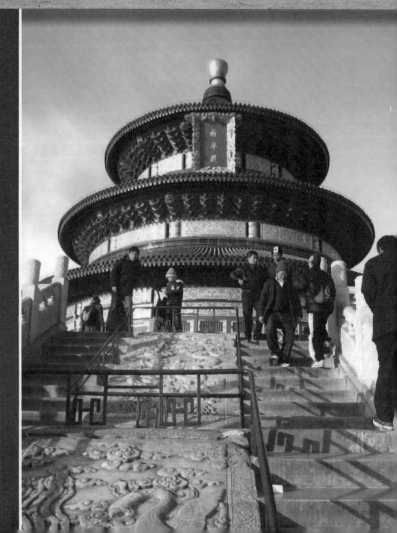

124 Terracotta Warriors

According to archaeologists, the terracotta army is a part of an elaborate mausoleum created to accompany the first Emperor of China Qin Shi Huang into his afterlife.

The terracotta warriors and horses were accidentally discovered when some farmers began to dig for a well at the foot of Mt. Lishan in China in 1974. They found thousands of clay soldiers each with a unique facial expression and positioned according to their positions. More excavations revealed swords, arrows and other weapons. Historically, these clay soldiers acclaimed to have the same status as the pyramids of Egypt and the sculptures of Greece!

125 The Red Fort

Lal Quila, also called the **Red Fort** is one of the most important historical monuments of India. This magnificent structure stands on the bank of River Yamuna and is made of red stone. The fort was built by Shahjahan, the Mughal Emperor who is also credited to have made the famous Taj Mahal in 1648.

Some remarkable buildings inside the fort are the Diwan-i-Am ('Hall of Public Audience') and the Diwan-i-Khass ('Hall of Private Audience'). Diwani-i-Khass is a highly-ornamented pillared hall, consisted of the legendary 'Peacock Throne' which was carried away by the Persian invader Nadir Shah.

126 The Three Gorges Dam

China's **Three Gorges Dam** is the world's largest dam and the also the largest hydroelectric dam based on generating capacity. The reservoir helps to control flooding on the Yangtze River basin. Dr. Sun Yat-Sen, the pioneer of the Republic of China, in 1919 first proposed the idea of the Three Gorges Dam. The cost of this project was about US$30 billion.

127 Topkapi Palace

When Istanbul was conquered by the Ottoman Turks in 1453, Mehmet II, the Conqueror, did not take over the Byzantine Palaces. Instead, he built his own palace where the main buildings of Istanbul University now exist. In 1459, Sultan Mehmet began to build the **Topkapi Palace** which had the Harem and the fourth courtyard. 6 years later, the rest of the palace was built. The Topkapi Palace functioned almost as an autonomous entity like a city within a city.

128 Tosho Gu Shrine

Tosho Gu Shrine was built in 1617 as a mausoleum for the shogun Tokugawa Leyasu, who put an end to the Sengoku civil war period. 15,000 craftsmen worked for two years continuously, using 2.5 million sheets of gold leaf to build this. Shinto shrines, are characterized by minimum architecture. But Toshogu has a riot of colours, and carvings.

129 Varanasi

Varanasi, also known Banaras, is located on the banks of the Ganges River in Uttar Pradesh, a state in India. It is the world's oldest living city. The city is considered the most sacred place for all Hindus.

Varanasi has the finest river frontage with miles of steps for religious bathing. It is full of temples and palaces which rise tier on tier from the water's edge. Varanasi was the capital of the kingdom of Kashi during the time of the Buddha. It is famous for its silks and brocades with gold and silver threadwork.

130 Wailing Wall

The **Wailing Wall** is a portion of the surviving wall of the Temple Mount in Jerusalem. In 70 CE, it was destroyed by the Romans. The Temple was the centre of the spiritual world. The world was filled with awe of God at the time when the temple stood. History says that Jerusalem was destroyed and rebuilt nine times. And through it all, one symbol remained intact, the Western Wall!

As God had promised that the Jewish people will never be destroyed, similarly, the 'Wall' has become a symbol of the Jewish people who can never be harmed. They will outlive their enemies and remain eternal.

131 Wat Arun

Wat Arun, is situated on the west bank of the Chao Phraya River. It is considered to be one of the most outstanding temples in Thailand due to the beauty of its architecture and the fine craftsmanship. The spire of Wat Arun is one of Bangkok's world-famous landmarks. It's spire which is 70 m high is beautifully decorated with tiny pieces of coloured glass and Chinese porcelain. Wat Arun looks absolutely stunning at sunset, particularly when lighted up at night.

132 Aitutaki Atoll

Aitutaki Atoll is a coral island or islands that encloses a lagoon partially or completely. The Aitutaki Lagoon in the Cook Islands is one of the most beautiful island lagoons in the world. The islets are also called 'motu'. It is situated in the middle of the South Pacific Ocean with thousands of kilometres of open sea from any mainland or continent. Aitutaki Atoll is volcanic in origin and rises to about 140 m above the sea level. Its 12 offshore islets, however, are low coral formations. A reef encircles the entire island with an enclosed lagoon. The average annual rainfall exceeds 1,900 mm with occasional droughts.

133 Bora Bora

Bora Bora is the most mythical of the Pacific islands. Honeymooners and romantics think that Bora Bora is unique with its water bungalows and it offers an enchanting environment. The island is adorned with lush tropical slopes, perfect white-sand beaches with emerald waters.

Bora Bora is a small island and can be circled by car in about an hour. To the southeast of the island is the Coral Garden, a natural underwater park where all types of fish and corals are found. Bora Bora lagoon offers a multitude of activities and excursions, one of the most popular being the Shark feeding.

134 Devil's Marbles

Devil's marbles are huge red-coloured boulders or rocks in the Tennant Creek region of Australia's Northern Territory. They hold tremendous significance for the aboriginal people. These rocks are huge blocks which are 1.7 billion year old granite rounded by countless centuries of weathering.

The Devil's Marbles began forming about 1700 million years ago when a layer of molten magma was deposited below a layer of sandstone and was cooled into granite with the passage of time.

135 Great Barrier Reef

The **Great Barrier Reef**, near the coast of Queensland in Australia, is the world's largest reef system. It is made up of more than 2,900 individual reefs and 900 islands extending over 2,600 km. It creates a natural water break between the immense waves of the Pacific Ocean and the coast of Australia. It is larger than the Great Wall of China!

The Great Barrier Reef is made up of

billions of tiny organisms called coral polyps. It is the world's largest natural collection of corals. Four hundred coral species, both hard corals and soft corals are found on the Great Barrier Reef. The reef was declared a World Heritage Site in 1981.

136 Lord Howe Island

Lord Howe Island is a remarkable example of isolated oceanic islands, born of volcanic activity under the sea. These islands are very proud of its magnificent topography and are home to numerous endemic species, especially birds.

The Lord Howe Island's southerly coral reef and its spectacular scenic landscapes enclosed within a small land area, provides important breeding grounds for colonies of seabirds. It is also an important natural habitat for the conservation of threatened species.

137 Milford Sound

Milford Sound is located in the south west of New Zealand's South Island. Although, it is called a 'sound', it can be termed as a fjord. It is situated within the Fiordland National Park, Milford Sound and runs 15 km inland from the Tasman Sea. It is surrounded by sheer rock faces that rise 1200 m on either side. Among the peaks are The Elephant at 1517 m which resembles an elephant's head, and Lion Mountain, 1302 m, in the shape of a crouching lion. Lush rain forests cover the cliffs, while seals, penguins, and dolphins fill the waters.

138 Pinnacle Desert

The Pinnacles are limestone formations located within Nambung National Park, near the town of Cervantes, in the Pinnacles Desert, Western Australia. Thousands of huge limestone pillars rise out of a landscape of yellow sand. At some places they reach up to three and a half metres tall. Some are jagged, sharp-edged columns, rising to a point; while others resemble gravestones.

The raw material for the limestone of the pinnacles came from sea shells created by marine organisms. These shells were broken down into lime-rich sands which were brought ashore by waves and then carried inland by the wind to form high, mobile dunes. The Pinnacles are thus the eroded remnants of the formerly thick bed of limestone.

139 Uluru

Uluru, also called Ayers Rock, is an 'island mountain', an isolated leftover left after the slow erosion of a large mountain range located in the southern part of central Australia. It is a large sandstone rock and is one of the oldest rocks on Earth with most of its bulk below the ground, and measuring 9.4 km in circumference.

It was formed over a period of about 500 million years! Uluru is famous for appearing to change colour as sun-light strikes it at different times of the day and year from different angles. Although, rainfall is uncommon in this area, whenever it rains the rock acquires a silvery-grey colour.

140 Dunedin Railway Station

The magnificent Victorian **Dunedin Railway Station** is one of the most famous buildings in the South Island of New Zealand. It is located in Dunedin and on the departure point for the Taieri Gorge Railway service which provides passengers with breathtaking views of the river gorges and the mountains.

The foundation stone for this unique railway station was laid in 1904 and it opened in 1906.

The hall for booking has a mosaic floor made of nearly 750,000 Minton tiles. A frieze of Royal Doulton porcelain runs

around the balcony above it. Various art shops on the station's first floor exist nowadays.

141 Sydney Harbour Bridge

The **Sydney Harbour Bridge** is one of Sydney's most well-known landmarks. The bridge took 8 years to get constructed (including the railway line) and was finally completed in 1932. This bridge is known popularly as the 'Coat Hanger'.

The Harbour Bridge was officially opened for public on March 19, 1932. The total

cost of the bridge was approximately 6.25 million Australian pounds. The bridge was built by 1400 workers. One should take on a Bridge Climb while at Sydney. It's an unforgettable experience and it gives a rare glimpse of the Sydney cityscape.

142 | Sydney Opera House

The **Sydney Opera House** which has a unique architecture is in Sydney, Australia. It is one of the most well-known performing art centres in the world. It was inaugurated in 1973. The opera house has a performing arts complex with a concert hall with the capacity of 2680 and an opera with1550 seats. There are playhouses and studios inside the Opera House with many bars and restaurants. A wide range of performances are staged here like symphonic music, opera, theatre and ballet. In 2007, it was designated a UNESCO World Heritage Site.

143 Amalfi Coast

The **Amalfi Coast** is a popular tourist destination in Italy. The Amalfi Coast is a stretch of coastline on the southern coast of the Sorrentine Peninsula in the Province of Salerno in Southern Italy. This beautiful shoreline stretches about 50 km along the southern side of the Sorrentine Peninsula. The Amalfi Coast is one of Europe's most breathtaking coastlines.

The Amalfi Coast is known for its production of limoncello liqueur as the area is a known cultivator of lemons. It is also a known maker of a hand-made thick paper which is called *bambagina*.

144 Aran Islands

The **Aran Islands** are a group of three islands that exist at the mouth of Galway Bay, on the west coast of Ireland. It takes just 40 minutes from the mainland to reach the desolate beauty of the Aran Islands.

Apart from their natural beauty, Aran Islands are famed for their cultural heritage. They are a perfect spot to experience Irish culture, and traditional Irish music. The Aran Islands consist of three islands – Inis Mór , Inis Meain and Inis Oirr. Inis Mór is the largest of the three and is well-known globally.

145 Azure Window

The **Azure Window** is a natural arch featuring a table-like rock over the sea in the Maltese island of Gozo. It was created millions of years ago when two limestone caves collapsed.

The arch of the Azure Window is, however, slowly disintegrating. Large pieces of rock keep falling from the arch. It is expected that the arch will completely disappear within just a few years. The arch is in a dangerous condition and warning notices are placed to stop people walking over the top of the arch. Once the arch has completely crumbled away, the Azure Window shall be renamed Azure Pinnacle.

146 Blue Grotto

Capri **Blue Grotto**, known as 'Grotta Azzura' in Italian, is a world famous natural cave located on the isle of Capri. It is famous for its magical, shimmering, intense blue tones and the magical silvery light which comes from the objects immersed in its waters. The effect is created by the daylight coming in the cave through an underwater opening located below the entrance of the cave. The entrance to the cave is very small, about 1 m high above the sea level, and visitors are required to lie down in the boat while the boatman rows the boat inside through the passage.

147 Capri

Capri is an enchanting and picturesque island made of limestone rock. It is in the Bay of Naples, in the south of the city of Naples and near the tip of the Amalfi Peninsula. The island is in the Mediterranean Sea.

In the olden times, the island of Capri was a favourite with Roman emperors, the rich and famous, artists, and writers. The island's top attraction is the famous Blue Grotto. Around the whole island, beaches are scattered. There are only two towns here— *Capri* and *Anacapri*, the higher town.

148 Cascate del Mulino

Cascate del Mulino is a natural wonder where a steaming hot spring water comes out of the ground at 37.5 C and cascades over a series of small waterfalls and into dozens of pools at various consecutive levels. It is in Saturnia, a small town in the municipality of Manciano in Maremma, Italy. It is located on a hill overlooking the famous thermal springs.

There are two outdoor waterfalls, the **Cascate del Mulino** and **Cascate del Gorello**. The Cascate del Mulino is considered to be the most famous natural springs in Tuscany. The waterfalls are made of several natural pools of warm thermal water. They are open to public and are free throughout the entire year.

149 Caves of Aggtelek Karst and Slovak Karst

Aggtelek Karst and Slovak Karst is a vast karst landscape of limestone plateaus which has more than 700 caves. It is the home to the world's highest stalagmite. This is the most extensively explored karst area in Europe.

The 21km Baradla-Domica cave connects Hungary-Slovakia. The Gombasek cave is probably the more photographed, with its impressive rock formations. These caves are also noted for having the world's highest stalagmite which is 32.7 m tall!

All these karst landforms are the result of long term geomorphological processes which are typical of this temperate climatic zone.

150 Cliffs of Moher

The **Cliffs of Moher** situated in Ireland rise to a height of 203 m. They are completely vertical and the cliff edge abruptly falls away into the constantly raging sea waters. The cliffs take their name from an old fort called Moher.

The cliffs mainly consist of beds of Namurian shale and sandstone. It is seen that 300 million year old river channels cut through it. It has been estimated that 30,000 birds live on the cliffs, consisting of 20 species. These include Atlantic Puffins, which live in large colonies at isolated parts of the cliffs and on the small Goat Island. Some other birds are hawks, gulls, guillemots, shags, ravens and choughs.

151 Davolja Varos

Davolja Varos in a unique rock formation in the Radan mountains in the region of southern Serbia. Together, there are about 202 distinctive rock towers or columns that rise into the air. It is believed that these towers have been created by erosion. People visiting this area can also see two different natural springs— Djavolja Voda and Red Well.

152 Eisriesenwelt Cave

The **Eisriesenwelt** which is a German word for 'world of the ice giants', is a natural limestone ice cave located in Werfen, Austria inside the Hochkogel mountain in the Alps. It is the largest ice cave in the world, covering more than 42 km. It is visited by about 200,000 tourists every year. However, only the first km, the area that visitors are allowed to visit, is covered in ice. The rest of the cave is formed of limestone.

Depending upon the outside temperature, it is either warmer or cooler inside the mountain.

153 Finisterre

Cape Finisterre is a rocky peninsula on the west coast of Galicia in Spain. The name *Finistère* derives from the Latin *Finis Terræ*, meaning '*end of the earth*'. Finisterre is primarily dominated by miles of hilly and broken coastline with high, towering cliffs, hidden coves and tiny ports which occupies France's northwest tip.

Cape Finisterre has some spectacular beaches, including O Rostro, Arnela, Mar de Fora, Langosteira, Riveira, and Corbeiro. The largest population of Finistère exists in Brest.

154 Fjords of Norway

Since times unknown, Norway has always been known for its scenic beauty of fjords, mountains and glaciers. **Fjords** can be defined as a very thin, long, and narrow bay in a valley made by the glaciers.

The Fjords of Norway have been carved out by glaciers from the hard-rock coastal mountains. The resulting narrow fjords are walled in by incredibly steep cliffs, verdant slopes and snow-covered mountain tops. The Fjords of Norway has attracted visitors from across the globe.

155 Frozen Sea

Luleå is the capital of Swedish Lapland. This isn't the only place in the world where the sea freezes, but the town's location jutting out into the sea forms a unique holiday destination. It makes the frozen water a welcome extension of the town's streets in the cold winters. From the months of December to February, the local people snow-trek and sled across the bay, and across the sea. Walking on the frozen water is a completely normal winter pastime in northern Sweden. Lakes and rivers as well as the sea between Sweden and Finland are turned into roads, cross-country ski tracks!

156 Gateway to Hell

The pass Námaskarð in Iceland maybe called '**The Gateway to Hell**'. Iceland is one of the world's most volcanically active countries, and it is indeed ironical considering its chilly name.

The pass Námaskarð is strategically located at a short distance from the Krafla volcano system as well as other interesting geological spots like Búrfellshraun and the desert Mývatsöræfi. One may also find a number of fumaroles, mud pools and mud pots that all seem to be boiling endlessly.

When the colonists arrived in Iceland, they thought of this volcano as the gateway to hell!

157 Iceland

Iceland, often called 'the land of ice and fire', is a volcanologists' paradise. The island itself was created due to a large volcanic hot spot sitting on a mid-oceanic ridge, in a unique setting.

Iceland has many active volcanoes. It has 30 active volcanic systems, of which 13 have erupted since AD 874. The volcanic eruption which was the most dangerous in Iceland's history was the so-called Skaftáreldar meaning 'fires of Skaftá' in the year 1783-84.

158 Jeita Grotto

Jeita Grotto are underground limestone caves which were inhabited in prehistoric times. They lie 18 km northeast of Beirut, and they attract countless visitors with their vivid colours and stalactite formations. The biggest stalactite in the world is located here.

159 Jungfrau-Aletsch-Bietschhorn

Jungfrau-Aletsch-Bietschhorn is one of the most glaciated areas in the Alps. This area includes Europe's largest glacier and a range of unique features resulting from glacial activity some of which are U-shaped valleys, cirques, horn peaks and moraines.

Despite the fact that much of the site is covered by glaciers, snow and rock, there are several forests and vegetation zones.

Animals that live there include the chamois, the alpine ibex, the red deer and the roe deer. Other common mammals include the mountain hare, fox, ermine, weasel, stone marten, and marmot.

160 Lauterbrunnen Valley

Lauterbrunnen Valley in Switzerland is said to be the most beautiful valley in all Europe. It lies deep in the Swiss Alps. It is a deep cleft cut in the landscape running between steep limestone precipices. It is a U-shaped valley (the world's deepest) with cliff on either side rising 1000 m, doused by some 72 waterfalls! The Staubbach Falls, one of Europe's highest unbroken waterfalls which falls from a height of 270 m lies here.

161 Matala Caves

In the central south coast area of Crete lies a small village called **Matala**. It's famous for its caves, which form the backdrop to a picturesque beach. In the ancient Minoan times, Matala was most probably the port for the Palace of Phaistos, which lies about 10 km north of the village. Today the Matala Caves are protected by the Archaeological Service. During the summer this ancient site is full of buses and rental cars. But in winter, Matala becomes a ghost town.

162 Mount Etna

Mount Etna is one of the most active volcanoes in the world. It is actually an active stratovolcano on the east coast of Sicily. Towering above the city of Catania on the island of Sicily, it has been growing for about 500,000 years! Mount Etna is 3.048 m high. It is the highest mountain in Italy. More than a quarter of Sicily's population live on Etna's slopes. Their main source of income comes from agriculture and tourism. The fertile volcanic soils support extensive agriculture. The slopes are rich in vineyards and orchards.

163 Mount Vesuvius

Mount Vesuvius is said to be a dangerous volcano due to the fact that about 3,000,000 people live near it.

Mount Vesuvius is one of history's most famous volcanoes. It is roughly 1310.6 m high. It is a deadly volcano located near the Bay of Naples, in the region of Campania, in Italy. The eruption that happened on August 24 A.D. 79, destroyed the cities of Herculaneum, Stabiae, and Pompeii. This made Vesuvius famous. Pompeii was buried 3.048 m under the volcanic material that was thrown out by the eruption of the volcano, while Herculaneum was buried under 22.86 m of ash. Pompeii and Herculaneum remained buried until the 18th century.

164 Plitvice Lakes

Plitvice lakes is a series of shallow lakes in the heart of Croatia. They are a paradise nature lovers with clear waters pooled in between rocky canyons and dramatic waterfalls gushing over cliff edges.

Wooden walkways have been made which makes access easy for visitors. Swimming is prohibited inside the national park, but there are places for a dip outside, such as Korana Village.

The lakes are famous for their distinctive colours, ranging from azure to green, grey or blue. About 8 km of pathways and wooden walking trails have been made around the lakes which make them accessible to visitors.

165 Pulpit Rock

Pulpit Rock or Preikestolen, is one of the most incredible tourist attractions in Norway. The natural rock formation with a 25 m squared plateau stands tall at 604 m above the sea! People suffering from vertigo should never visit this place as it is a 604 m drop from a flat plateau down to Lysefjord with no safety railings.

166 Seljalandsfoss Waterfall

Seljalandsfoss is a unique waterfall in the river Seljalandsá, about 30 km west from Skógar. It falls from a height of 60 m and has a path behind it at the bottom of the cliff, but with a thin cascade! It is the only known waterfall where it is possible to walk behind it. Though there are countless waterfalls in the world, this particular waterfall is very picturesque. It serves as Iceland's prime attraction.

This beautiful and awestriking waterfall can be reached from the farm of Seljaland along the Ring Road, Iceland's main highway.

167 Skaftafell National Park

Skaftafell National Park, Europe's largest national park is formed over millions of years by volcanic eruptions, rivers and glaciers and it has a variety of striking landscapes. It is Iceland's second national park, established in 1967.

This exotic national park gets 160, 000 visitors per year who come to admire the thundering waterfalls, twisted birch forests, the numerous intertwined rivers and the lurching tongues of ice. The unique natural beauty of this park is a result of favourable weather conditions which creates the interplay of fire and ice.

168 Stonehenge

Stonehenge is undoubtedly Britain's greatest national icon. The ancient megaliths of Stonehenge and Avebury speak clearly of the engineering skills of the ancient people who made them and whose identity is still unknown. Stonehenge began about 3000 B.C. as a circular earthen bank and adjacent ditch.

The Stonehenge World Heritage site spreads over 26.6 square kilometres. Archaeologist Alexander Keiller excavated and re-erected many stones in the 1930s. He also founded an archaeological museum on the site.

169 Stromboli

Off the coast of Sicily, **Stromboli** is a small volcanic island with several hundred brave inhabitants. It is one of the most active volcanoes on Earth and has been erupting almost continuously since 1932. It is constantly spewing lava fountains, gas and ash. It is indeed fascinating for volcanologists but scary for common people. It is among the world's most visited volcanoes.

As the eruptions are so distinctive, the geologists use the word 'Strombolian' to clearly describe similar eruptive activity at other volcanoes. The base of Stromboli begins over 1000 m below the surface of the Tyrrhenian Sea and it rises to an elevation of 924 m above sea level.

170 The Giant's Causeway

The **Giant's Causeway** is one of Ireland's biggest natural attractions. The Giant's Causeway lies at the foot of the basalt cliffs along the sea coast on the edge of the Antrim plateau in Northern Ireland. The causeway consists of some 40,000 massive black basalt columns sticking out of the sea. They look as though they've been created by human beings rather than nature.

This unique, dramatic sight has inspired legends of colossal giants striding over the sea to Scotland. Geologists opine that these formations was caused by volcanic activity during the Tertiary Period, some 50–60 million years ago!

171 Verdon Gorge

The Gorges du Verdon in France, also called the Grand Canyon du Verdon, is a spectacular natural wonder. It is 700 m deep, 21km long canyon which varies in width between 6 and 100 m at the bottom and 200 to 1500 m at its rim.

Although it's much smaller than Arizona's Grand Canyon and should not be compared, the Gorges du Verdon is deep, compact, wild and beautiful.

The sparkling turquoise waters of the Verdon River flow through this beautiful gorge of Europe.

172 Wadden Sea

The **Wadden Sea** is a large temperate, relatively flat coastal wetland area in Germany. It is formed by the intricate interactions between physical and biological factors that have given rise to numerous transitional habitats which include tidal channels, sandy shoals, sea-grass meadows, mussel beds, sandbars, mudflats, salt marshes, estuaries, beaches and dunes.

The Wadden Sea is home to numerous plant and animal species, including marine mammals such as the harbour seal, grey seal and harbour porpoise. It is also a breeding and wintering area for up to 12 millions birds per annum and it supports numerous other species. The Wadden Sea is one of the last remaining natural, intertidal ecosystems on earth today.

173 Wielierka Salt Lines

Wieliczka Salt Mine, which is located 10 km from Krakow, is one of Poland's most popular tourist attractions. It was listed by UNESCO as a World Heritage Site in 1978.

This unique mine was built in the 13th century and it produced table salt continuously until 2007. It is considered as one of the world's oldest salt mines which is still working.

The major attractions of this mine include dozens of statues, three chapels and a complete cathedral that has been carved out of the rock salt!

Europe (Manmade Wonders)

174 Acropolis

The **Acropolis** of Athens is an ancient citadel on a high rock. It is one of the most well-known Greek historical sites in the world. It stands tall above Athens, and contains a number of buildings and monuments. They include the Parthenon, the Erechtheion, the Propylaia and the Temple of Athena Nike.

Most of the sites on the Acropolis were constructed in the 5th Century BC, which was known as the 'golden age' of Athens. These sites have managed to survive through invasion, conquest and war over the passing centuries.

175 Altamira Cave Paintings

The **Altamira cave paintings** found in Spain are one of the greatest collections of ancient art ever discovered. The cave was discovered by a hunter in 1868. The cave has 296 paintings. The paintings depict bison, red deer, boar and horses.

The passages of the cave are twisting and its chambers are shaped like the alphabet 'S'. Altamira has been listed by UNESCO World Heritage Site in 1985.

176 Arc de Triomphe

The **Arc de Triomphe** is one of the most famous monuments in Paris and was built in 1806 after the victory at the Battle of Austerlitz by Emperor Napoleon I. It was built in honour of those who fought for France, during the Napoleonic Wars. Inside, on the top of the arch is engraved the names of the generals and the wars fought. The Arc de Triomphe is 49.5 m tall, 45 m wide and 22 m deep. The vault is 29.19 m high and 14.62 m wide.

177 Avila Walls

Avila, the Spanish city is located 53 miles northwest of Madrid. It is the highest city in Spain and is best known for its tall, majestic walls that surround the city. These walls are among the longest and the best-preserved walls in the world. They were built in the 11th and 12th centuries. The walls are 2.5 km long, 12 m high and 3 m thick. There are about 88 towers and nine gates in this long wall.

178 Basilica Di San Francesco

The gorgeously decorated Basilica of St. Francis in Assisi appears to be rather unsuitable for a man who preached and lived a simple life of poverty and abstinence.

Brother Francis died in Assisi on October 3, 1226. Within two years, plans were made for the construction of a church in his honour. The main part of the lower church was completed by May 25, 1230, when the *body of St. Francis* was transferred to its new resting place.

179 Basilica Notre Dame

Notre-Dame Basilica is a basilica in Montreal, Canada. The church's Gothic architecture is a dramatic characteristic that is most noticeable. The interior of this basilica is grand and colourful. Its ceiling is deep blue in colour and decorated with golden stars. The rest of the building is a work of many colours like blues, azures, reds, purples, silver, and gold. It is filled with hundreds of intricate wooden carvings and several religious statues.

180 Baxia

Baxia is considered to be an example of Europe's first urban planning with broad squares and pedestrian streets. It lies in the heart of Lisbon. It is the main shopping and banking area.

The place has a strange charm with old tramcars, street performers, decorated pastry shops, and street vendors selling everything from flowers to souvenirs.

181 Berchtegaden

Berchtesgaden is a district located in the German Bavarian Alps. Berchtesgaden is located in the south district of Berchtesgadener Land in Bavaria, 180 km southeast of Munich.

Berchtesgaden is full of myths and legends. It enjoys an unusual natural beauty in abundance. It is framed by six mountain ranges and is the home to Germany's second-highest mountain, the Watzmann.

182 Big Ben

One of London's best known landmarks is **Big Ben**, the Clock Tower of the Palace of Westminster. The clock inside the tower was the world's largest when it was installed in the middle of the 19th century. The clock is known for its accurate timings as it has rarely failed during its long life span. Big Ben looks extremely beautiful at night when the clock faces are illuminated.

183 Bone Chapel

The 'Capela dos Ossos' or 'Chapel of Bones' is a well-known monument in Évora, Portugal. It is a small chapel located next to the entrance of the Church of St. Francis. This chapel is unique and gets its name because the interior walls are covered and decorated with human skulls and bones! The skulls and skeletons got from the centuries of war and plague victims, all form the unusual and creepy artwork of this chapel.

184 Bremen Town Hall

The old Town Hall of Bremen built in the Gothic style in the early 15th century is the seat of the President of the Senate and Mayor of the Hanseatic City of Bremen. This old town hall stands as one of the most important examples of Brick Gothic architecture in Europe. It stands in the market square with the statue of Roland right in front of it. On the west side of the square the sculpture The Town Musicians of Bremen by Gerhard Marcks is displayed. Along with the statue of Bremen Roland, the town hall was added to the list of UNESCO World Heritage Sites in July 2004.

185 British Museum

The **British Museum** began when Sir Hans Sloane a physician, naturalist and collector, had handed down a collection of 71,000 objects to King George II in return for a large payment. King George II readily accepted the grant in 1753 and established the British Museum.

For the general public the British Museum was opened on January 15, 1759. The number of visitors has increased from 5,000 per year to 6 million today!

186 Buckingham Palace

The **Buckingham Palace** in Westminster, England, is the official London residence of the British Queen. It takes its name from the house built for John Sheffield, Duke of Buckingham.

Buckingham Palace has 775 rooms. These include 19 state rooms, 52 royal and guest bedrooms, 188 staff bedrooms, 92 offices and 78 bathrooms. The palace has a sprawling garden. This area includes a helicopter landing area, a lake, and a tennis court.

187 Burgos Cathedral

Burgos Cathedral is a Gothic cathedral located in northern Spain. It is famous for its colossal size, rich Gothic architecture, and a very significant history. This beautiful cathedral was ordered to be constructed by King Ferdinand III and Mauricio, the English-born Bishop of Burgos. The construction started on 1221 and was completed in nine years! Burgos Cathedral was designated a World Heritage Site by UNESCO on October 31, 1984.

188 Canals of Venice

Venice is a unique city built on 118 small islands. It holds a special place because of its canals. The canals date back to the 5th century. The city has about 150 canals and the most important canal is called the 'Grand Canal'. The traffic of Venice is managed through these canals. The total length of the Grand Canal is 3 km. The Grand Canal is bordered on either side by palaces, churches, hotels and other public buildings. Water buses and water taxis ply as means of transport.

189 Canterbury Cathedral

The **Canterbury Cathedral** of Canterbury in Kent is one of the oldest churches in England. It was originally founded in AD 602 by St. Augustine. The cathedral has been listed in the UNESCO World Heritage Site. The cathedral exhibits elaborate carvings in English Gothic style. There is a majestic collection of medieval stained glass windows as well. The importance of this medieval cathedral was enhanced by the murder and canonization of Archbishop Thomas Becket in the premises of the cathedral.

190 Castel Sant' Angelo

Castel Sant' Angelo is in Rome, Italy on the River Tiber. It was constructed as a tomb for Emperor Hadrian during the 2nd century BC. This unique building was converted into a military fortress in the mid 6th century. In 1901, it was converted into a museum. Castel Sant' Angelo got its name from the statue of the archangel Michael that decorates the building.

191 Catacombs of St. Calliixtus

The Catacombs of Rome are ancient underground burial under or near Rome, Italy. Rome has some of the oldest and longest burial underground tunnels in the world. Some of these tunnels are well-known and open to visitors, while others are seldom explored. Many catacombs must have been lost too. Initially, the catacombs were not that large. But they grew larger and larger around the tombs of saints because people asked to be buried near them.

192 Chambord Chateau

The **Chateau de Chambord** is one of the most well-known manor houses in the world located in Chambord, Loir-et-Cher, France. It is a perfect and unique example of French architecture. This chateau was made by King Francois I as he wanted to be near to his mistress the Comtesse de Thoury, Claude Rohan, wife of Julien de Clermont, who lived nearby.

The Chambord's hugeness bears testimony to the fact that it has 440 rooms, 84 staircases and 365 fireplaces! The castle also has eleven kinds of towers and three kinds of chimneys. This remarkable castle is surrounded by a large wooded park.

193 Channel Tunnel

The **Channel Tunnel**, also called the 'Eurotunnel', is a rail tunnel between England and France that runs beneath the English Channel. This unique tunnel, which is 50 km long, consists of three tunnels; two for trains and a central tunnel for services and security. The tunnel is used for both goods' vehicles and passenger vehicles.

The project of building this tunnel was jointly done by France and England. Digging began on both sides of the Strait of Dover in 1987–88 and was completed in 1991. The tunnel was officially inaugurated on May 6, 1994.

194 Charles Bridge

Charles Bridge is a 14th century bridge linking the two sides of Prague. It is made of stone. This awe striking structure is one of the city's finest attractions. Charles Bridge is full of people during the day. There are artists and musicians who are particularly entertaining. There are now 75 statues on Charles Bridge, though most are copies, as natural calamities over the centuries have damaged the originals.

195 Chateau de Chenonceau

Château de Chenonceau is one of the most visited royal residences in France. This magnificent medieval château was constructed by Thomas Bohier and his wife Katherine Briçonnet. This castle was owned by a number of kings. The castle's entrance displays all of the 'coats of arms' of the first royal owners of the place.

Château de Chenonceau houses an enormous library. It also has several large halls that can entertain hundreds of visitors. The beautiful garden adds beauty to the castle. Visitors leave the place with a fairy tale feeling.

196 Colonge Cathedral

The **Cologne Cathedral** is the greatest Gothic cathedral in Germany. It is dedicated to Saints Peter and Mary. Cologne Cathedral is proud to have the world's largest church façade.

This awe striking cathedral houses a major treasure—a golden reliquary containing the remains of the Three Magi of Christmas story fame. Due to these relics and other treasures, this cathedral has become a major pilgrimage destination in the Christian world. Construction of this Gothic church began in the 13th century and it took, more than 600 years to get completed!

197 Colosses of Rhodes

The Statue of Colossus in ancient Rhodes is one of the Seven Wonders of the Ancient World. It was 9.14m tall. It was a gigantic statue of God Helios. It was erected by the sculptor Chares of Lindos. This mighty statue was built in memory of the defeat of the Roman Army, which was trying to take control of Rhodes.

198 Colosseum

The **Colosseum** is an amphitheatre in Rome where gladiators met in combat and prisoners fought with wild beasts in front of bloodthirsty crowds! The Colosseum was built by Emperor Vespasian in AD 69–79.

The Colosseum was made of concrete, marble and limestone. It was capable of seating 50,000 spectators! It is the largest amphitheatre to have ever been built in the Roman Empire and was oval shaped.

199 Cuenca Old Town

Cuenca, is an exquisite town in central Spain. This town is considered to be unique as it is perched on a rock formation sided by the gorges of two rivers. The town is famous for its hanging houses. The houses date back to the 14th and 15th centuries. Cuenca has a number of monuments and rivers. It is also listed in the UNESCO World Heritage Site for its monuments.

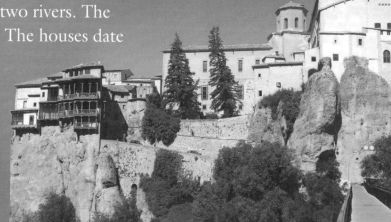

200 Delphi

Delphi is one of the most important archaeological sites of Greece. It was the seat of the Oracle in ancient Greece. Since the Oracles could predict the future, most of the kings and common people used to consult the Oracle on important matters. Delphi has attracted visitors since many years and it does now also. Some important sites that should be visited in Delphi are the famous Temple of Apollo, the Tholos, the Delphi Museum and the Charioteer of Delphi. Delphi was included in the UNESCO World Heritage Site in 1987.

201 Deutches Museum

Located in Munich, Germany, the **Deutsches Museum** is the world's largest technology and science museum. The museum is visited by approximately 1.5 million visitors per year. The museum boasts of exhibiting about 28,000 objects from 50 fields of science and technology.

Located in the centre of the town on an island in the Isar River, the museum opened amidst much celebration in 1925.

The Deutches Museum covers topics such as aerospace, agriculture, chemistry, computers, electricity, marine navigation, mining, music, railways, astronomy, and telecommunication.

202 Dionysus Theatre

The ancient **Theatre of Dionysus** is in Athens, Greece. It is regarded as the first sample of Greek theatres and it is considered to be the birthplace of the Greek drama. This well-known ancient theatre was dedicated to Dionysus, the Greek God of wine making and ecstasy.

The works of ancient Greek stalwarts of drama like Aeschylus, Aristophanes, Euripides and Sophocles were acted here. It was the world's first theatre built of stone. It is believed that around 15,000 to 17,000 spectators could sit in the theatre together!

203 Doge's Palace

The Palazzo Ducale or **Doge's Palace**, was the centre of the Venetian government for centuries. It was also the venue for its law courts, its civil administration and bureaucracy until its relocation across the Bridge of Sighs — the city jail. This important palace was once occupied by a 10th century wooden stockade. This stockade had watch towers and moat which was eventually destroyed by fire and other disasters.

Sala del Maggior Consiglio is probably the most magnificent hall in the Doge's Palace. It has frescoes by Veronese and Tintoretto.

204 Dubronik

Dubrovnik is a beautiful city on the Adriatic Sea coast of Croatia. It is often called the 'the pearl of the Adriatic'. It is one of the most prominent tourist destinations on the Adriatic. Dubrovnik joined the UNESCO list of World Heritage Sites.

Dubrovnik is very special. Magnificent walls run around the marble streets and baroque buildings. It is rich in Renaissance and Baroque churches, monasteries, palaces and fountains. Beyond the city, nature offers a rich landscape with beaches, wooded peninsulas and a sea dotted with lush islands.

205 Eiffel Tower

The **Eiffel Tower** which was once the tallest structure in the world is the best known landmark of Paris. It was built for the 'World Exhibition' in 1889 which was held in celebration of the French Revolution of 1789.

It was the world's tallest tower at 320 m, until it was eclipsed by Manhattan's Chrysler Building some four decades later. The Eiffel Tower designed by one called Gustave Eiffel who was well-known for his revolutionary bridge building techniques. The structure took more than two years to complete.

206 Epidaurus

The Theatre of **Epidaurus** in Greece is well-known for its excellent sound system. This famous theatre was built in the 4th century BC by Polykleitos the Younger. It had 35 rows of seats divided into 34 blocks by stairs and walkways.

It is said that if a pin is dropped at the centre of the orchestra, one can hear it hit the ground from any where in the theatre! This amazing theatre is still in use today. Actors come from all over the world to perform there.

207 Florence Cityscape

The city of **Florence** in central Italy is situated on the top of a river called Arno and is well-known for its interesting history, art and architecture.

Florence has attracted tourists mainly because of its cityscape. Some of the major attractions of the city are the *Duomo, the city cathedral, the Florentine skyline, the Loggia dei Lanzi*, and many more. The Florence Cityscape is famous for its artistic past. Many great Italian artists belonged to this city. During the evening, the city lights up like a beautiful painting. Most visitors to Florence come mainly to experience the

history and the culture of this magnificent Italian city. The City of Florence was declared a World Heritage Site since 1982.

208 Frederiksborg Castle

The **Frederiksborg Palace** is situated on three islets in the Castle Lake in Hillerød. It is situated to the north of Copenhagen, Denmark. The palace was designed and built in Dutch Renaissance style by King Christian IV in the 17th century.

The beautiful gardens which surrounds the palace has been built in the Dutch Renaissance style. The Museum of National History at Frederiksborg Palace houses quite a good collection of portraits, historical paintings and modern art.

209 Gaudi Sacred Family Church

Antoni Gaudí's Basilica and Expiatory Church of the Holy Family, or Sagrada Família is located at Barcelona, Spain. The church is the most popular tourist attraction in the city, with over two million visitors a year! The church was largely unfinished when Gaudi died in 1926. The construction of the church began in 1883 and is still incomplete!

210 Golden Lane

Golden Lane is one of the most interesting locations in Prague. It was originally known as Goldsmith's Lane as many goldsmiths lived here. Some of them were more of alchemists than goldsmiths. The row of houses in this small street is one of the most picturesque locations in Prague.

Many years ago, the Golden Lane had smaller dwellings, which eventually fell into disrepair. Then, one by one they were replaced by houses we see today. Presently, most of these small houses have shops which offer their goods such as books, lace and the famous Czech glass products. The street has a strange fascinating atmosphere. The famous writer Franz Kafka lived here with his sister for a few weeks in the house number 22.

211 Gothic Quarter

The **Gothic Quarter** in Barcelona is an incredible old world filled with ancient castles and churches. Some of these date back to 15 B.C. during the times of the Roman Emperor Augustus. A visitor goes back through the ages while walking through the narrow cobblestone alleys, turrets, walled courtyards and Corinthian columns where the Kings once reigned. Some of the remarkable buildings of this extraordinary place are *Cathedral de la Seu, the Royal Palace* and the *Picasso Museum*.

212 Heidelberg City

Heidelberg is said to be one of the most beautiful cities of Germany. It lies in the south-west of Germany and forms a part of the densely populated Rhine-Neckar Metropolitan Region. This unique city is a harmonious combination of castles, old town and river nestled in the hills of the Odenwald. The enchanting beauty of the city has attracted thousands of tourists since long and will do so in future.

The city has the oldest university of Germany which was established in 1386. This university has a history of over 800 years. Heidelberg in the present times forms the centre of Germany's science and research.

213 Herculaneum

Herculaneum was an ancient city in Campania, Italy with 4,000–5,000 inhabitants. It was located 8 km southeast of Naples, near the base of Mount Vesuvius. It was sadly destroyed together with Pompeii, Torre Annunziata, and Stabiae by the Vesuvius eruption of AD 79. In the year 1997, collectively, the ruins of Pompeii, Herculaneum, and Torre Annunziata were declared a UNESCO World Heritage site

This ancient city of Herculaneum was connected with the name of the Greek hero Heracles in the ancient tradition. It was a clear indication that the city was of Greek origin.

When the first discovery of ruins occured in 1709, there were important finds of the magnificent Villa of the Papyri with a big library, and bronze and marble statues, a basilica with fine murals, and a theatre.

214 Hofburg Palace

The huge **Hofburg Palace** is the most important building in Vienna, the capital of Austria. It was once the centre of the powerful Habsburg Empire. This palace has served some of the most powerful people in European and Austrian history. This huge and beautiful palace was built between the 13th and the early 19th centuries. Today, the Hofburg Palace houses various museums and a library, as well as the offices of the Austrian President.

215 Imperial War Museum

The **Imperial War Museum** is in London. The museum was founded in 1917 to keep a record of Britain's war efforts. It also displays materials relating to World War I. In the year 1939, the museum started collecting items from the World War II also. The museum's collections include archives of personal and official documents, photographs, video recordings, military vehicles and aircrafts related to wars.

216 Karelia

Karelia is the area between Finland and Russia. The surface area of this republic is largely broad, flat, and swampy. Kizhi, is an island within Karelia. The visitors are awestruck by seeing the State Kizhi Museum made up of nearly 90 wooden structures! The wooden structures include chapels, windmills, and granaries. The most remarkable structure here is the Church of the Transfiguration of Our Savior built without a single nail!

217 Knossos Palace

The Minoan Palace at Knossos is remarkable as it is the largest and the most glorious of all Minoan Palaces in Crete. It is also known as the residence of the legendary King Minos, the famous judge and legislator. The Minoan Palace was built of ashlar blocks, has many floors and was beautifully decorated with frescoes. The old palace was built around 2000 B.C but was destroyed by an earthquake in 1700 B.C. The newer, and the more complex palace was built almost immediately after the first one was destroyed.

218 Kremlin and Red Square

The **Kremlin** in Moscow is the centre of the Russian government. It dates back to 1156 and contains a collection of impressive monuments. Some of them are the *Church of the Annunciation, Cathedral of the Dormition, Church of the Archangel* and *the Bell Tower of Ivan Veliki*. It is also the city's most important and most visited places.

The Red Square is closely associated with the Kremlin. It lies beneath its east wall. In the Red Square stands the famous Cathedral of St Basil the Blessed, one of the most beautiful monuments of Orthodox art.

219 Kunsthistorisches Museum

The **Kunsthistorisches Museum** (Art History Museum) in Austria was built in 1891 to house the extensive collections of the imperial family. Due to its vast collection of art works, it is considered to be one of the most eminent museums of the world. The collection is one of the most significant of its kind and proudly displays the precious artworks from the Middle Ages, the Renaissance and the Baroque era.

220 La Scala

La Scala, is a well-known opera in Milan, Italy. It is one of the principal opera houses of the world. The theatre was inaugurated on August 3, 1778 and was originally known as the 'New Royal Theatre at La Scala'. Built in 1776–78 by the Empress Maria Theresa of Austria, it replaced an earlier theatre that had burned. The house was closed during World War I. The theatre reopened in 1946. In the present times, the theatre is recognised as one of the leading opera and ballet theatres of the world.

221 Latin Quarter

The **Latin Quarter** which is a major tourist attraction in Paris, is located on the bank of the Seine River, France. The importance of this area is generally associated with artists, intellectuals, and a bohemian way of life. Latin Quarter has many monuments, museums and gardens. Some of them are the Musée de cluny or the Muséum National d'Histoire Naturelle and the Institut du Monde Arabe.

222 Le Puy-En-Velay

Le Puy-en-Velay, a major Christian pilgrimage town, is in France. A red cast-iron statue of about 15 m high of 'Our Lady of France' was placed in 1860 on a hill. At the base of the hill stands the Romanesque Cathedral of Notre-Dame. Le Puy-en-Velay is the beginning point of the 1600 km walking pilgrimage to Santiago de Compostela in Spain. It also has a lot of other religious shrines. One of them is Saint Michel d'Aiguilhe's Chapel.

223 Leaning Tower of Pisa

Leaning Tower of Pisa is located in the seaside town of Pisa, in the Tuscany region. Although, the tower started to lean before it was even finished due to loose soil and bad foundation, the tower become an architectural splendour after completion.

This unique tower has eight floors and is 55.7m tall. The tower is made out of white marble. The construction of the tower began in August 1173 and continued for about 200 years. It is indeed a mystery that the name of the architect is yet unknown.

224 Louvre Museum

The **Louvre Museum** in the French capital of Paris is the largest, the oldest and the most well-known museum in the world. The museum is laid out into four sections or wings. At the heart of the Louvre Museum is the Carosel de Louvre where the famous glass pyramid stands. The museum also houses many of the most famous pieces of artwork of human history. At the top of this list is the famous painting of Mona Lisa by Leonardo da Vinci. Today, the grand museum contains more than 300,000 works of art including the works of Raphael.

225 Madame Tussaud's Wax Museum

Madame Tussauds is often thought to be 'London's favourite tourist attraction'. It is a wax museum with branches in a number of major cities. It was founded by a wax sculptor named Marie Tussaud. The eye-catching replicas at Madame Tussauds Wax Museum have been thrilling its visitors since its inception in 1835.

This unique museum brings together many well-known figures made of wax from the fields of history, politics, entertainment, royalty and history.

226 Malta and Gozo

It has been observed that the oldest buildings in Europe are found in Malta. They are older than the Pyramids of Egypt! The stone temples on these small Mediterranean islands of Malta and Gozo go unnoticed nowadays. But during the time as far back as 5000 B.C., they used to draw hordes of worshippers. 'Hagar Qim', the most impressive of the temple complex, attracts attention from its hilltop location on Malta's southern coast. It was constructed from enormous limestone slabs. Hagar Qim's best statues were excavated in the mid 20th century. Now, they are safely preserved in Valletta's National Museum of Archaeology.

227 Medici Chapel

The **Medici Chapel** was constructed to house the tombs of Giuliano and Lorenzo de' Medici. It is located in the New Sacristy of the Church of San Lorenzo in Florence, Italy. It contains the tombs of members of the Medici family. Michelangelo and his students had designed and built these monumental structures between 1520 and 1534. Though the Medici Chapel was never completed, it is the only one of Michelangelo's great architectural-sculptural creations. In 1534, after Michelangelo left for Rome, the sculptures in the chapel were placed by his students.

228 Meteora Monastries

The **Meteora Monastries** are in a place called Thessaly in Greece. The word 'Meteora' in Greek means 'suspended in the mid air'. It is famous for the monasteries on top of tall rocky hills. During the fearful period of political instability which occurred in the 14th century Thessaly, the monks of that time had begun building monasteries on top of these inaccessible peaks. By the end of the 15th century there were 24 of them.

The Meteora was designated the World Heritage Site in the year 1988. Today, only four monasteries exist.

229 Mezquita of Cordoba

The **Mezquita of Cordoba** is a magnificent building in the Spanish city of Cordoba. Though it is a cathedral today, but the majority of its art and architecture has an Islamic flavour as it was build as a mosque in the 8th century.

During the times of Abd ar-Rahman II, the Amir of Cordoba, the Mezquita contained an original copy of the Koran and an arm bone of the Prophet Mohammed, making it an important Islamic pilgrimage site.

230 Milan Cathedral

The **Milan Cathedral** which stands on the main square of Milan city is the largest Gothic cathedral and the second largest Catholic cathedral in the world! This gorgeous and large cathedral dates back to the 14th century and took 500 years to complete! The tallest spire of the cathedral is decorated with the statue of Madonna. The cathedral can accommodate up to 40,000 people at a time!

231 Mont St Michel

Mont-St-Michel is a small rocky island about 1 km from the north coast of France. The mount is best noted for the medieval Benedictine Abbey and steepled church that fills most of the 1km-diameter clump of rocks jutting out into the English Channel.

This uniquely located church is connected to the mainland with a thin natural land bridge. Climbing to this church is hard. A maze of rooms, staircases, and vaulted halls make up the abbey.

232 Mount Athos

Mount Athos is a peninsula in Halkidiki in northern Greece. This area is considered to be sacred and it contains twenty monasteries including one Serbian, one Bulgarian and one Russian. By a law called 'avaton', female visitors are not allowed to enter the monastery. Only adult men and young males accompanied by their fathers are permitted to enter Mount Athos.

233 Mycenae

The ancient archaeological sites of **Mycenae** form an important part of the Mycenaean civilization. It is situated upon a small hill-top. This city is intrinsically linked to the Homeric epics, the *Iliad* and the *Odyssey* which form an important part of the classical Greek literature. The site was first excavated in the year 1874 by Heinrich Schliemann, a German amateur archaeologist. Visitors can still see the remains of stone walls, underground tombs and the Lion Gate.

234 Mykonos

Mykonos is undoubtedly one of the most charming towns on a beautiful island in Greece. The island looks just like a picture-postcard with its little white house, hand-painted streets, windmills, chimneys, pigeon keepers, and numerous small churches. All the houses are painted white and have brightly coloured shutters in front of the windows. They are mostly painted blue, green and red. The village goes steeply up the hill. The narrow streets are always buzzing with activity and are lined with attractive small shops.

235 National Gallery

The **National Gallery** is in London. This gallery has one of the finest collections of Western European paintings around the year 1250 and onwards. Its masterpieces include the works of Botticelli, Titian, Raphael, Michelangelo, Caravaggio, Rembrandt, Cezanne, Hogarth, and Gainsborough.

This remarkable gallery contains more than 2300 paintings! Van Gogh's famous 'Sunflowers' and John Constable's 'The Hay Wain' are displayed here. The gallery organizes touring exhibitions in cities throughout Britain apart from offering courses and lectures.

236 Neuschwanstein Castle

The **Neuschwanstein Castle** located in Bavaria, Germany is one of the most frequently visited castles in Germany. It is also one of the most popular tourist destinations in Europe. It was built by King Ludwig II of Bavaria in the year 1869 but could not be completed due to his death. Neuschwanstein literally means 'New Swan Castle'. The castle has a beautiful inner garden surrounded by a walled courtyard. It even has an artificial cave. This unique castle inspired Walt Disney to create the magic Kingdom.

237 Newgrange

One of the finest European passage-tombs is **Newgrange**. Built on the top of a small hillock in Ireland. This tomb was discovered accidentally in 1699. Newgrange was originally built about 3100 BC but it stands in a restored form even today. It consists of a vast stone and turf mound measuring 85 m in diameter and 13.5 m in height. It contains a passage leading to a burial chamber. Outside this, 38 large boulders up to 2.4m high form a ring.

238 Nîmes Amphitheatre

Nîmes in France houses the famous **Nîmes Amphitheatre**. It was built at the end of the 1st century. Originally, this amphitheatre at Nîmes was used for serious purposes not for entertainment. It had once been a fortress sheltering thousands of destitute people. But today, it is used primarily for exciting bullfights. It consists of two levels of 60 arches each. Inside this, more than 20,000 spectators could attend the fights of the gladiators.

239 Nymphenburg Palace

Nymphenburg Palace was built from 1664 as a summer residence for Elector Ferdinand. Elector Ferdinand Maria and his wife Henriette Adelaide of Savoy appointed architect Agostino Barelli to build them a summer residence in the west of Munich in order to celebrate the birth of their son and heir. This remarkable palace is situated at the centre of a park landscape amidst a network of canals. This unique palace is still owned by the Wittelsbach family, the royal family of Bavaria. About 65 people work here in the various departments. The palace with its buildings and gardens stretch over 0.03 km.

240 Old City of Strasbourg

The **City of Strasbourg** is the capital of the region of Alsace is located on the Franco-German border. The city's history and culture has been shaped by both countries throughout the centuries. The uniqueness of this city lies in the fact that it has a medieval and village-like charm along with a modern flavour.

The city of Strasbourg is divided by the Ill River, which divides and surrounds the Big Island on which the old town and most of the city's famous buildings are located. The island was designated a UNESCO World Heritage site in 1988.

241 Olympia

Olympia is remembered even today as the birthplace of the Olympic Games and as the sacred site of Zeus. It is a ruined sanctuary of Greece. Olympia is richly endowed with many treasures of Greek art. It is full of temples, altars, theatres, monuments, and statues of brass and marble. The Temple of Zeus was the largest and most important building at Olympia. It was designated a UNESCO World Heritage site in 1989.

242 Opéra Garnier

The **Opéra Garnier** was the world's largest theatre and opera house when it was initially opened. It stands royally in Paris, France and was opened in 1875.

On January 8, 1875, the first opera was performed here. The building was designed by Charles Garnier, one of the jewels of Napoleon III and it took 14 years to complete. It also has a vast stage with space for 450 artists. The opera has a seating capacity of 2200 people.

243 Paestum

Paestum is the classical Roman name of a major Greco-Roman city. It lies in the Campania region of Italy. Paestum was mainly discovered due to the three Doric temples. These temples though roofless, are still standing! The smallest of the three temples standing on a small platform was dedicated to Athena. It is also known as the Temple of Ceres. The oldest of the temples was the Temple of Hera. But the most well-preserved is the Temple of Neptune or Poseidon.

244 Palace of Versailles

The **Palace of Versailles** is in Versailles, France. In French, it is known as the Chateau de Versailles. Under Louis XIV, this palace was changed from a hunting lodge into an extravagant palace surrounded by gardens. It became the seat of the French government. One of the most remarkable rooms in the palace is the 'hall of mirrors'. The room is so named because light from 17 windows on one side of the room is reflected by the corresponding arched mirrors on the opposite wall! The palace is also adorned with lovely pieces of art and chandeliers as well.

245 Pamplona

Pamplona is the capital city on the Navarre Province, Spain. It is famous for the 'San Fermin fiesta' that happens every year from July 6th to 14th. This unique festival features the running of the bulls across the streets. The bulls are made to run all over the town with adventurous people trying to dodge them!

246 Pantheon

The **Pantheon** in Rome is the most preserved and influential building. It is a Roman temple dedicated to all the Gods of pagan Rome. It was built by Marcus Agrippa and rebuilt by Emperor Hadrian in AD 126. The Pantheon for many ages has been noticed for its remarkable size and design. In AD 609, the temple was converted into a Catholic Church. At the top of the dome is a large opening, the oculus. This was the only source of light.

247 Piazza dei Miracoli

Piazza dei Duomo, also called **Piazza dei Miracoli** is located at the north of the Arno River in Pisa, Italy. The Piazza dei Miracoli is set over a lush green field, surrounded by four masterpieces of Medieval art— the renowned Leaning Tower, the Camposanto (the graveyard), the Baptristy and the Cathedral itself. It is a perfect combination of architecture and sculpture placed around a wide tender green lawn.

248 Pompeii

In ancient times, **Pompeii** was a Roman city, buried by a volcanic eruption. It was located on a plateau formed by an ancient lava deposit southeast of the volcano Mt. Vesuvius. The inhabitants of this lost city did not know that Mt. Vesuvius was a volcano. 2000 years later, archaeologists uncovered this city buried under the earth. The unfortunate people in ancient Pompeii did not have a chance to escape after the massive eruption. When archaeologists dug out the city two thousand years later, they found hardened bread still in the ovens that had been baking that day!

249 Portofino

Portofino is a small, pretty Italian village famous for fishing. The village is located on the banks of an Italian River and it is extremely picturesque. It has a lot of small harbours and is said to be the most beautiful Mediterranean ports. The high cliffs which are trees lined, the blue ocean, the warm sunny weather, along with delicious food, makes Portofino a perfect holiday spot.

250 Prado Museum

Prado Museum, is an art museum in Madrid, which houses the world's richest collection of Spanish painting, as well as other European masterpieces. The museum opened for the first time on November 10, 1819. The museum's collection was enlarged by private donations.

The museum contains the masterpieces by Titian, Bosch, Botticelli, Rembrandt, Fra Angelico, El Greco, Velázquez and Francisco de Goya.

251 Prague Old Town Square

The **Old Town Square** of Prague forms the heart of this city located in the Czech Republic. It is surrounded by magnificent buildings in different architectural styles. Some of the historical buildings are the Old Town City Hall, St. Nicholas Church and Tyn Church and Kinský Palace. The Astronomical Clock which dates back to the 15th century is another important building.

It displays, besides time, the astrological positions of the moon and the sun.

252 Reichstag

The **Reichstag**, the centre of the German Parliament, is one of Berlin's most historic landmarks. This immensely important building was constructed between 1884 and 1894. In the year 1933, a massive fire broke out in the building destroying much of the Reichstag. By 1970s, the building underwent partial restoration and was converted to a German museum of German history.

253 Rhodes Old Town

Rhodes Old Town is in Greece. With a population of 6,000 inhabitants, this city is surrounded by medieval walls with seven gates. The walls are 4 km long. They surround both the palace and the town. The most interesting part of the Old City is the 'Street of Knights', the most important street of the medieval town. The Palace of the Grandmaster is one of the most impressive site in Rhodes. The old town was designated a UNESCO World Heritage Site in 1988.

254 Rock of Cashel

The **Rock of Cashel** located in Ireland is one of its most spectacular sites. The 'Rock' is a green hill, full of limestone outcrops. It rises from a grassy plain on the edge of the town and is full of ancient fortifications. An enclosure circled by sturdy walls contains a complete round tower, a 13th century Gothic cathedral and the finest 12th century Romanesque chapel in Ireland. Rock of Cashel was a symbol of power and the seat of kings and churchmen who ruled over the region for more than 1000 years.

255 Romantic Road

The **Romantic Road** is in Bavaria, Germany. This unique road takes us through a variety of walled medieval towns, majestic castles and lush green countryside in Bavaria. The road starts from Wurzburg and ends at Fussen. The road also passes by the famous Neuschwanstein Castle!

256 Ronda

The city of **Ronda** is located in the north western part of the province of Málaga and is surrounded by mountains. Ronda is one of the oldest cities in Spain. It is easily accessible by car, bus and train. It houses Spain's oldest bullring which is a stone Neoclassical structure. It is a museum now. Ronda is surrounded by national parks.

257 Royal Palace

The 'Palacio Real' or **Royal Palace** in Madrid is supposedly the largest and certainly one of the most magnificent palaces of Europe. It has more than 2000 luxuriously decorated rooms out of which only 50 can be visited. The palace dates back to the 18th century and exhibits beautiful artwork. The Royal Palace is the official residence of the present king but he does not live there. The palace is however used as a museum.

258 Salamanca Old Town

Salamanca is one of Europe's most beautiful Renaissance cities located in Spain. The city has a number of sandstone buildings that gives a golden glow. Due to this it is often called 'the golden city'. It is also well-known as it houses one of oldest universities of Europe. The Salamanca Old Town was designated a UNESCO World Heritage Site in the year 1988.

259 Salisbury Cathedral

The **Salisbury Cathedral** is an Anglican cathedral in Salisbury, England. It was formally known as the 'Cathedral Church of the Blessed Virgin Mary'. This cathedral is considered to be one of the most significant examples of early English architecture. The main part of the cathedral was completed in 38 years. The cathedral has the tallest church spire in the United Kingdom which is 123 m. The cathedral also has the largest cloister and the world's oldest working clock.

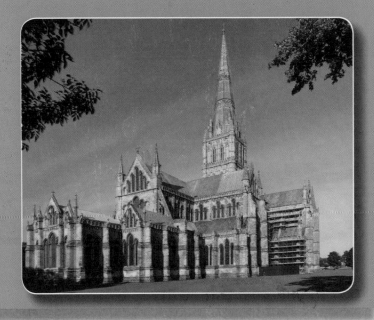

260 San Gimignano

San Gimignano is a medieval town in Tuscany, Italy. It was originally called the 'City of Silva'. San Gimignano is a perfect city to feel the civilization of the Middle Ages as it is full of medieval squares, wells and fountains, streets, houses and palaces. San Gimignano was designated a UNESCO World Heritage Site in 1990.

261 San Vitale Basilica

The **Basilica Di San Vitale** in Ravenna built in the 6th century contains what are probably the finest Byzantine mosaics of Europe. Its construction was started by Ecclesois, the Bishop of Ravenna. The basilica is noted for not only its mosaics but also its Byzantine architectural style. It has an octagonal plan. Two of the finest mosaics notably feature the Byzantium Emperor Justinian and his wife Theodora.

262 Santa Maria Delle Grazie

The **Santa Maria delle Grazie** is one of Milan's most well-known churches. This particular church's fame rests on Leonardo da Vinci's fresco on 'Last Supper'. This extremely precious painting shows Jesus with his 12 apostles. The painting was begun in 1495 and was painted on a plastered wall inside the church. Santa Maria delle Grazie has been designated a UNESCO World Heritage site in 1980.

263 Santorini

Santorini is a small, circular group of volcanic islands located in the Aegean Sea. It is about 200 km south-east from the mainland of Greece. It has a giant central lagoon and is surrounded by high steep cliffs on three sides. The island of Santorini is noted for its unique architectural designs. It is not only the ideal holiday delight offering its visitors relaxation but also has a taste of adventure and romance.

264 Schönbrunn Palace

Schönbrunn Palace is a former summer residence of the Austrian kings which is located in modern Vienna in Austria. The palace has been one of the major tourist attractions in Vienna. Schönbrunn Palace was built by Emperor Maximilian II in the mid 16th century.

The palace has 1,441 rooms but only 40 are open to visitors. In ancient times, some 1,000 people lived in the palace. The gold ornamentation, frescos, ceilings, mirrors and chandeliers are all in plenty here. The gardens of the Schönbrunn Palace are unusually beautiful. They are a combination of French garden, English garden and botanical garden.

265 Segovia Aqueduct

The Roman aqueduct of Segovia situated in the city of Segovia, is probably one of the most well preserved buildings of the ancient world. This Roman aqueduct carries water for 16 km from the Frío River to the city of Segovia, Spain. The impressive structure was built under the Roman Emperor Trajan. The part of the aqueduct above the ground is 728 m long and consists of some 165 arches at a height of 9 m.

266 Sistine Chapel

The **Sistine Chapel** is located in the Vatican City. The chapel is famous for its Renaissance frescoes by Michelangelo. It was designed to be the pope's chapel and the site of papal elections. Today, the building forms a part of the museums of the Vatican. The chapel has a rectangular shape. This well-known chapel was designed by the architect called Giovanni dei Dolci. The frescoes on the ceiling depict incidents from the Old Testament.

267 Spanish Steps

The **Spanish Steps** in Rome are a very special set of stairs. It connects the Piazza di Spagna Monti with the church Trinita dei Monti. These steps are special as they are the longest and widest steps in whole Europe! The steps date back to the 18th century. They attract tourists as well as locals who gather there. Francesco de Sanctis had designed the steps and were built between 1723 and 1726.

268 St. Basil's Cathedral

Popularly known as St. Basil's, this legendary building is actually a Russian Orthodox Church in the Red Square in Moscow. Officially, it is called 'The Cathedral of the Intercession of the Virgin by the Moat'. The cathedral was ordered by Ivan the Terrible to mark the 1552 capture of Kazan from the Mongol forces. The cathedral was completed in 1560. Initially, when it was built, it was all white to match the white-stone Kremlin, and the onion domes were gold rather than multi-coloured and patterned as they are today.

In the 17th century quite a few things were added to the cathedral like a hip-roofed bell tower and the gallery. In the year 1860, the Cathedral was repainted with a more complex and integrated design which remains unchanged till date. The Cathedral is now a museum. On the Day of Intercession in October, one service a year is held in the Cathedral.

269 St. Mark's Basilica

St. Mark's Basilica is the name of a church in Venice. This basilica is one of the finest examples of Byzantine architecture. It is known for its opulent designs and gilded interior mosaics. It is often nicknamed as the 'Church of Gold'. It was built in the 11th century and has been the seat of the Archbishop of Venice since 1807. The church was built to house the relics of St. Mark the Evangelist. These relics were supposedly stolen by Venetian merchants from Alexandria, many years ago.

270 St. Peter's Basilica

Situated in the Vatican City, **Saint Peter's Basilica** is the world's largest church and the centre of Christianity. This marvellous structure took more than 100 years to be constructed. The ancient Basilica was constructed by Emperor Constantine in the area where Saint Peter had been martyrized with the other Christians.

The interior of the church is full of Renaissance and Baroque art. Among them most famous are Michelangelo's Pietà, the baldachin by Bernini over the main altar, the tomb of Urban VIII, the statue of St. Longinus and the bronze cathedral of St. Peter in the apse.

271 St. Peter's Square

Saint Peter's Square which is located in front of St. Peter's Basilica, is one of the best known squares in Vatican. It is an important gathering place for tourists visiting the Vatican City. In 1656, Gian Lorenzo Bernini was commissioned by Pope Alexander VII to create this square. The square is made up of two different areas. The first has a trapeziod shape and the second is used for is elliptical shape. The square is often used for public gatherings and ceremonies.

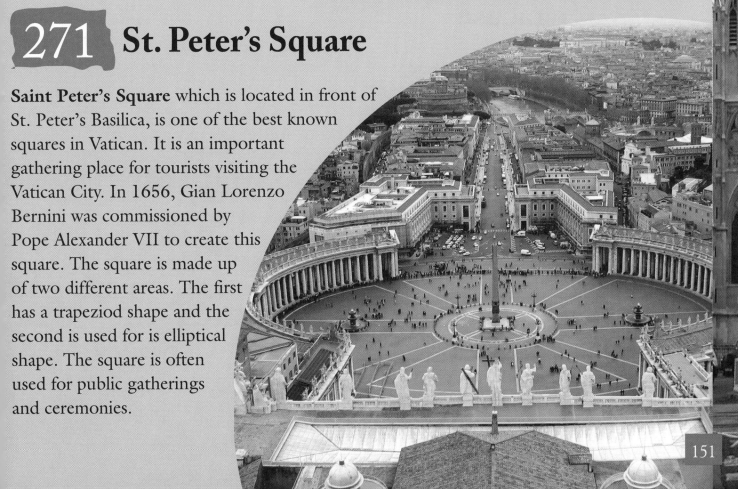

272 Statue of Zeus

The **Statue of Zeus** which stood at Olympia is one of the Seven Ancient Wonders of the World. It was sculpted by the Athenian sculptor Phidias around 435 B.C.E. The statue was made to honour the greatest Greek God and the father of the Olympic Games, Zeus.

This mighty statue was 12 m high and showed Zeus sitting majestically on his throne. The robe and ornaments of Zeus were made out of gold and he was made out of ivory. He also had a wreath around his head. In his right hand he held Nike his famous messenger and he held a rod with an eagle in his left hand. Unfortunately, the statue no longer exists.

273 Syracuse

Syracuse was established on the island of Sicily. It was once a mighty Greek colony. The place is full of Greek and Roman sites. This ancient city was built on an ancient Greek settlement founded by Conrinthians in 734 BC. Famous people like Archimedes, Pindar and Aeschylus lived in Syracuse. In the ancient times, it was one of the most important cities in Greece .

274 Temple of Poseidon

The **Temple of Poseidon** is located in Cape Sounion, Greece. What remains today of this sanctuary are mere ruins. It offers a wide view of the Aegean Sea and is close to the Greek Islands. The temple which was constructed in the honour of Poseidon, the Greek God of the Sea was built in 440 BC.

The design of the temple is a typical hexastyle that is it had a front portico with 6 columns. Only some columns of this ancient temple stand today.

275 The Pont Du Gard

The **Pont Du Gard** is a colossal bridge-aqueduct, well-known for its ancient Roman engineering work. It was constructed in about 1st century AD to carry water to the city of Nîmes over the Gard River in southern France. Pont Du Gard was constructed at the command of Augustus' son-in-law, Marcus Vipsanius Agrippa. The three tiers of arches rise to a height of 47 m. The first tier is composed of 6 arches, the second tier is composed of 11 arches of the same dimensions and the third, is composed of 35 smaller arches. Pont Du Gard was built without mortar like many of the best Roman constructions.

276 The Tower Bridge

London's **Tower Bridge** is one of the most important and recognizable bridges in the world. The bridge hangs over the Thames River in London, England. This iconic bridge was designed by Sir Horace Jones and was completed in 1894. The length of the bridge is 60 m. Its towers can rise to a height of 43 m. This is one of London's best-known landmarks.

277 Trevi Fountain

The **Trevi Fountain** is the most famous and the most beautiful fountain in all Rome. In 1732, Pope Clement XII had appointed Nicola Salvi to create a large fountain at the Trevi Square. This monumental Baroque fountain was finally completed in 1762.

Neptune, the God of the sea is the central figure of the fountain. He is riding a chariot pulled by two sea horses. One of the horses is calm and obedient, the other one restive. They symbolize the fluctuating moods of the sea. The light and shade effects on the marble, the tumultuous waves, create a magnificent scene.

278 Trulli District

Alberobello in Italy, the city of drystone dwellings known as *trulli*, is an exceptional example of mortarless construction. The trulli are made out of roughly worked limestone boulders. These unique dwelling areas were characterized by pyramidal, domed or conical roofs built up of corbelled limestone slabs.

Trulli are still being built today by specialist craftsmen and transformed into comfortable homes.

279 Vatican Museums

The **Vatican Museums** are located inside the Vatican City. These ancient museums are full of paintings, sculptures, and other artworks collected by the Popes over the centuries. The museums are full of architectural marvels like the *Sistine Chapel, the Chapel and Beato Angelico, the* *Raphael Rooms, the Loggia* and the *Borgia Apartment*. These historical museums celebrated their 500th anniversary in October 2006.

280 Vila d' Este

The **Villa d' Este** situated in Tivoli, Rome, with its palace and garden, is one of the most remarkable examples of Renaissance culture at its peak. Its inventive design along with the architectural components in the garden like the fountains, ornamental basins, etc. makes this a splendid example of an Italian 16th century garden.

281 Westminster Abbey

The **Westminster Abbey** is located in London. It is a Gothic monastery-church that forms the traditional place of coronation and burial for English monarchs. Some of England's most distinguished statesmen and famous people have been buried in the Abbey. Some of them were David Livingstone and Sir Isaac Newton. A part of the Abbey is known as 'Poets Corner' which includes the tombs of Geoffrey Chaucer, Ben Jonson, John Dryden, Robert Browning, and many others. Westminster Abbey was designated a UNESCO World Heritage Site in 1987.

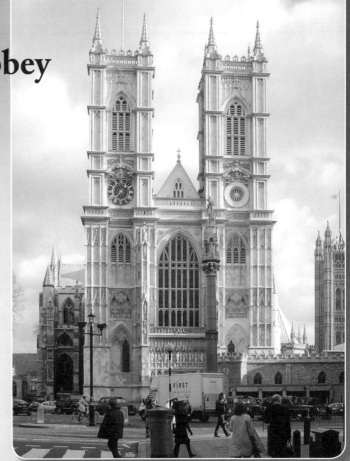

282 Windsor Castle

The **Windsor Castle** is the largest inhabited castle of the world. It is an official residence of The Queen. The Windsor Castle has been a Royal home for over 900 years, and it remains a working palace even today. The castle is located at Windsor, 22 miles west of London. It stands on a cliff above the River Thames.

283 Alcatrez Island

Alcatraz Island is located in the San Francisco Bay. The total area of the island is said to be 0.089031km². From November 1969, the island was occupied for quite sometime by a group of Aboriginal People from San Francisco. They were part of a wave of Native activism across the nation with public protests through the 1970s. In 1972 Alcatraz became a national recreation area and received designation as a National Historic Landmark in 1986.

Landmarks on the island include the Main Cell house, Library, Dining Hall, Lighthouse, the ruins of the Warden's House and Officers Club, Parade Grounds, Water Tower, Building 64, New Industries Building, Recreation Yard, and Model Industries Building.

284 Alejandro de Humboldt National Park

Alejandro de Humboldt National Park is a park located in north-eastern Cuba and covers most of the central part of the Saqua-Baracpa mountain range. The site of the park includes a complex system of mountains, tablelands, coastal plains, bays and coral reefs. Several rivers flow from the park.

The climate of the park has a hot, sub-tropical climate all year. Most rain falls between May and October and hurricanes can occur in autumn between August to November. Alejandro de Humboldt National Park has been nominated as the World Heritage site. It has a rich collection of animals — 10 species of mammals, 95 birds, 45 reptiles, 21 amphibians and 191 insects.

285 Arches National Park

Arches National Park, located in the desert country of Utah, contains the largest known concentration of natural stone arches in the world. The park contains more than 950 natural arches! It receives 750,000 visitors every year which justifies its popularity. Landscape Arch which soars 88 m through Utah's dry desert air is the highlight of the park.

286 Bay of Funday

The **Bay of Fundy** is one of Canada's best destinations. This Island is known as the largest Island of the Arctic Archipelago which lies directly in between New Brunswick and Nova Scotia which is in the East Coast of Canada. The bay has a funnel like shape.

The Bay of Fundy is 290 km in length. The mouth of the bay is 100 km wide. This bay is known for the rocks that are as high as a four storey building!

The second largest whale in the world, the finback whale is one of the residents of this bay. There are abundant fresh sea foods like fish, lobster, and mussels just to name a few.

287 Carlsbad Caverns

The **Carlsbad Caverns** are one of the world's oldest cave systems. It receives around 300,000 visitors per year! The caverns lie approximately 27 miles from the city of Carlsbad in the Guadalupe Mountains, New Mexico, beneath the Chihuahuan Desert. Carlsbad Caverns National Park was first designated a National Park on May 14, 1930. Carlsbad Caverns was also designated a UNESCO World Heritage Site on December 6, 1995.

This park was established to preserve Carlsbad Caverns. The park contains 83 separate caves, including the nation's deepest limestone cave measuring 486.8 m.

288 Cave of Crystals

A group of miners in the year 2000 working in the Naica mine, in the Mexican state of Chihuahua found an underground cavern containing giant selenite crystals which were mostly 11 m high. The enormous size and beauty of these gypsum crystals brought the cave to sudden fame.

In spite of its instant fame, the future of the cave is uncertain. Though access to the cave is currently possible for short periods, but the cave may be closed and flooded in the future to stop the crystals from breaking down.

289 Columbia Ice Fields

The **Ice field in Columbia** is located in the Canadian Rockies. The ice field lies partly in the northwestern tip of Banff and the southern end of Jasper National Park. It is about 325 km² in area, 100 m to 365 m in depth receiving up to 7 m of snowfall per year. The ice field feeds eight major glaciers.

290 Copper Canyan

The **Copper Canyon** of northern Mexico is one of the world's great natural wonders. It exists 965.6 km south of the Mexican border, is composed of a network of gorges which makes the canyon four times larger than the Grand Canyon! From snow-covered mountains to glassy lakes to breathtaking waterfalls to subtropical forests is seen in the Copper Canyon.

The Copper Canyon actually is made up of six great gorges, each forged by its own river. In some places, the Copper Canyon outgoes the depth of the Grand Canyon by more than 1,000 ft. The Copper Canyons are home to black bears, deer, predatory cats and plenty of lizards and snakes.

291 Crater Lake

The **Crater Lake** National Park is located in southwestern Oregon. This lake is known to be the deepest lake in the United States and the seventh deepest in the world! The Crater Lake partially fills the collapsed caldera of the ancient Mount Mazama Volcano. The caldera measured about 1219 m.

The Crater Lake is mostly filled with rain and melted snow. It is isolated from the streams and rivers that exist in the surrounding area. The lake is able to maintain its current level as the amount of rain and snowfall equals the evaporation and the rate of seepage.

292 Everglades

The Florida **Everglades** is one of the most extensive, complex, and well-known wetland ecosystems in the world. It is sometimes called the 'River of Grass'. The Everglades is really a long, shallow river nearly 80.5 km wide and more than 161 km long. It is home to a numerous variety of plants, animals, and birds—both permanently living there and also migratory.

Okeechobee, the second largest body of freshwater in the United States lies just north of the Everglades. The water from Okeechobee Lake and many other interconnected rivers, lakes, streams, flow into the Everglades. This combination of freshwater and salt-water systems creates the unique environment that formed the Everglades.

293 Giant Sequoia Trees

The giant forest of Sequoia National Park in California is the home for *Sequoiadendron Giganteum* or giant sequoia trees. The Giant Forest is the home of more than 8,000 colossal sequoia specimens. The largest of them all, the General Sherman Tree, is around 2,100 years old and weighs approximately 2.7 million pounds! It is almost 275 ft tall and has a trunk which is more than 30 m wide. General Sherman is considered to be the King of the forest. It is not only the largest living tree in the world, but the largest living organism on earth.

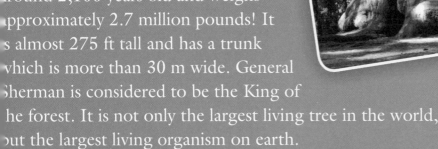

294 Grand Canyon

A canyon (also known as a gorge or a ravine) is a very deep valley with extremely steep sides, usually formed by the eroding action of a fast-flowing river.

The **Grand Canyon** is one of the largest canyons in the world, formed over billions of years by the Colorado River in the United States in the state of Arizona. It is 466 km long and approximately 29 km wide. The average depth of the Grand Canyon is 1,524 m. The deepest part of the canyon is 1,829 m.

Even though the Grand Canyon is not the biggest canyon in the world, it is known for its beautiful and complex landscape.

295 Great Blue Hole

A blue hole is a submarine cave or underwater sinkhole. They are also called vertical caves. They are roughly circular, steep-walled depressions, and so named for the stark contrast between the dark blue deep waters of their depths and the lighter blue of the shallow waters around them.

The **Great Blue Hole** is a large underwater sinkhole off the coast of Belize. It lies near the centre of Lighthouse Reef, 70 km away from the mainland. The hole is circular in shape, with a diameter of over 300 m and a depth of 124 m. The blue cave is perfect spot for divers because of its beauty.

296 Hawaiian Islands

The **Hawaiian Islands** are an archipelago consisting of eight major islands. It looks beautiful with its emerald green colour amidst the blue ocean. This archipelago consists of several atolls, numerous smaller islets, and undersea seamounts in the North Pacific Ocean. This extraordinary group extends 2,400 km. It is the birthplace of Barack Obama, the 44th President of USA. The Hawaiian islands are the seat of many volcanoes among which Kilauea is the most active. Tourists can visit this. It is called the world's only 'drive in volcano'.

297 Lava Tubes

Lava tubes are natural channels through which lava travels beneath the surface of a lava flow, thrown out by a volcano during an eruption. It maybe work either ways—lava could be actively draining from a source, or could be extinct, meaning the lava flow had stopped and the rock has cooled and left behind a long, cave-like channel.

Many a time, lava streams flow steadily in a confined channel for many hours, or many days sometimes for long distances like the 1969-74 **Mauna Ulu** eruptions at **Kilauea** in which the lava flows travelled underground through a lava-tube system for more than 7 miles long before it entered the ocean.

298 Mammoth Cave National Park

It is beneath the ridges of **Mammoth Cave National Park** in south central Kentucky, lies the most extensive cave system on Earth. A five-level cave system has been mapped, and new caves are continually being discovered. A 50 ft sandstone and shale cap acts as an umbrella over the limestone ridges.

This unique site of caverns is also a United Nations World Heritage site.

The cave ecosystem available in these caves is the world's most diverse. Approximately 130 forms of life can be found in Mammoth Cave. Most are quite small. Some are such specialized cave dwellers that they can live nowhere else! All are dependent on energy from the surface.

299 Meteor Crater

Meteor Crater, also called Barringer Meteorite Crater is bowl-shaped pit produced by a huge meteorite on the plain of the Canyon Diablo region 30 km west of Winslow, Arizona, United States. The crater is 1,200 m in diameter and about 180 m deep inside its rim.

The mighty crater was discovered in 1891, its age has been variously calculated between 5,000 to 50,000 years. Large number fragments of nickel and iron from the size of a gravel to 640 kg have been found in a 260 square-kilometre area.

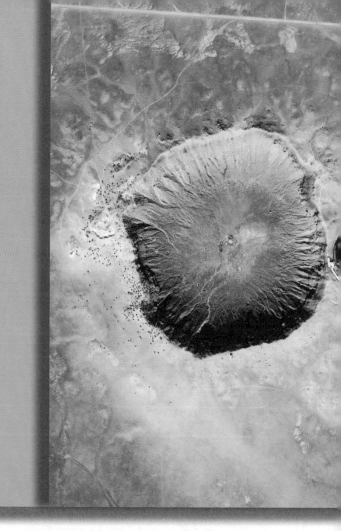

300 Moraine Lake Banff National Park

The **Moraine Lake** lies deep in the Canadian Rocky Mountains. The Moraine Lake along with its sister Lake Louise, is extremely picturesque and is one of the most photographed landscapes in Banff National Park.

It's known as the jewel of the Rockies for its deep crystalline greenish-blue waters that mirror pine forests, soaring mountains and the endless sky!

301 Na Pali Coast

Hawaii has plenty of breathtaking landscapes consisting of sandy beaches, giant waves and volcanic craters. But the beauty of the **Na Pali Coast** of Kauai, which is 17 km long may top them all. The lush green mountains stand tall with slopes and ridges for more than 1,300 m before dipping into the Pacific. The only land access to this marvellous area is via the Kalalau Trail that starts at Kee Beach.

302 Paria Canyon

The Paria River in northern Arizona has carved a smaller version of the Grand Canyon. The 112,500 acre uninhabited are has towering walls streaked with desert varnish, sandstone arches, wooded terraces, and hanging gardens. The **Paria Canyon** trail follows the river which is subject to periodic and seasonal flash flooding. Some of the rock formations, including 'The Wave', are just incredible.

303 Paricutin Volcano

Paricutin Volcano is situated in the city of Paricutin located 320 km west of the Mexico City. The volcano erupted on February 20, 1943. It is the fastest growing volcano ever recorded in history. It grew up to 45 m in just six days and 3,170 m tall in just 9 years. The Paricutin volcano is special because farmers actually saw it being formed. On February 20, 1943, Dionisio Pulido, a farmer, was in his field sowing. Suddenly, he felt a thunder rocking the ground beneath him. The ground nearby opened in a crack of about 46 m length. Slowly the ground was raised 2 m in height and along with it smoke or fine dust like ashes began to rise. The event was also accompanied with hissing and whistling sounds. A volcano had just been born right under a farmer's feet!

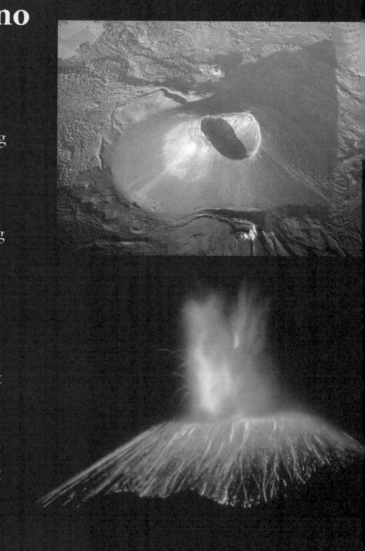

304 Percé Rock

Percé Rock, just off the tip of the Gaspé Peninsula is a massive rock which is 433 m long, 90 m wide and 88 m high rising from the Atlantic. It maybe called an Island in the Gulf of Saint Laurence in the province of Quebec. The island is a massive formation of rocks layered with lime stones. It is also called pierced rock because it has a hole in its structure which forms an arch like figure.

305 Redwood National Park

The **Redwood National Park** was established on October 2, 1968 by President Lyndon Johnson by combining the three existing state parks. He added more land and expanded the park. The Redwood National Park was created to protect the growth of coast redwoods, some of the world's tallest trees.

Three California state parks and the National Park are a World Heritage Site and International Biosphere Reserve protecting the natural resources cherished by the people of many nations.

Within the park, there are four developed campgrounds in the park system. Kayaking

is popular along the coastline. The local Yurok and Tolowa tribes perform traditional dance ceremonies throughout the year for the visitors.

306 San Andreas Fault

San Andreas Fault is a great fracture of the earth's crust in California. It is the main fault of an intricate network of faults extending more than 965 km from North-West California to the Gulf of California. The San Andreas Fault, which is a strike-slip fault, also extends vertically at least 30 km into the depths of the earth.

Many earthquakes have occurred along it, including famous ones in 1857, 1906 and 1989 earthquakes.

San Andreas is a complex zone of crushed and broken rocks. Many smaller faults branch from and join the San Andreas Fault zone.

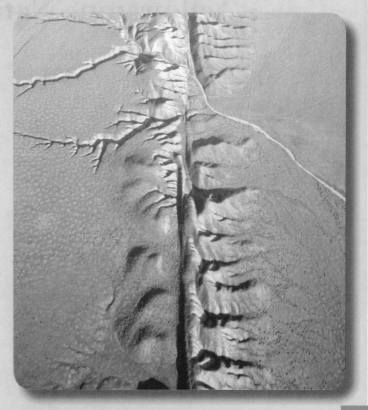

307 Sequoia National Park

Sequoia is the second-oldest national park of America. It lies in the southern Sierra Nevada and was established on September 25, 1890.

The Sequoia Park is famous for its giant sequoia trees, including the General Sherman tree, one of the largest trees on Earth. The General Sherman tree grows in the Giant Forest which contains five out of the ten largest trees in the world! This Giant Forest is connected to the Kings Canyon National Park's General Grant Grove, home of the General Grant tree which is one variety among other giant sequoias.

308 Yellowstone National Park

The **Yellowstone National Park** is the first national park of the world formed on March 1, 1872. It is located in the U.S. in the states of Wyoming, Montana and Idaho. The park is known for its wildlife and its many geothermal features, especially the Old Faithful Geyser.

The Park covers an area of 8,980 square km, including within lakes, canyons, rivers and mountain ranges. The Yellowstone Lake is one of the largest high-altitude lakes in North America and is cantered over the Yellowstone Caldera, the largest super volcano in the continent. Half of the world's geothermal (relating to heat present inside Earth) features are present in the Yellowstone Park. Lava flows and rocks from volcanic eruptions cover most of the land area of Yellowstone.

The most famous geyser in the park, and perhaps the world, is *Old Faithful Geyser*, located in Upper Geyser Basin. It erupts 'faithfully' after about every 65 minutes for about 4 minutes, which is why it got its name. The name 'Yellowstone' comes from the Yellowstone River, which in turn gets its name from the yellow coloured rocky cliffs located its banks in the northern region of the park.

309 Yosemite National Park

Yosemite National Park lies in the centre of California. With its hanging valleys, many, cirque lakes, polished domes, moraines and U-shaped valleys, the national park stand unique and incomparable. The park is dominated by the Sierra Nevada, which is a tilted granite area. Granite underlies most of the park.

Yosemite is gifted with exceptional natural beauty, including 5 of the world's highest waterfalls, a combination of granite domes and walls, deep valleys, alpine meadows, numerous giant sequoia trees, lakes, and a variety of species.

A lot of change has occurred in the Yosemite landscape. Suppression of natural fires and heavy sheep grazing has altered the original vegetation.

310 Zion National Park

Zion National Park in Southwestern United States, is one of the most exotic and spectacular places on our planet. It was created by many forces of Nature through millions of years. The Zion Park is a source of amusement, enjoyment and entertainment for more than 2 million people who visit it each year. The park was established in 1909. The Kolob Canyons section was added to the park in 1937. This park offers the breathtaking views of magnificient mountains, and trails and also offers infinite possibilities to explore and enjoy nature.

311 Acapulco

Acapulco is a port located in the Guerro state in southwestern Mexico. It is a popular resort city that has harbour on Mexico's pacific coast. Acapulco is one of the finest natural anchorages in the world. This port city is well-known for its explosive nightlife, picturesque beaches, unlimited water sports and the breathtaking view of the Acapulco Bay.

312 Brooklyn Bridge

The **Brooklyn Bridge** is considered to be one of New York's most well- known landmarks. This impressive bridge stretches between Brooklyn and Manhattan and it spans over a length of 1.8 km. It was constructed between 1869 and 1883. The bridge was designed by one called John Augustus Roebling. The most remarkable feature of the Brooklyn Bridge are the two masonry towers to which numerous cables are attached and with the help of which the bridge hangs.

313 Cabot Trail

The **Cabot Trail** is a highway and picturesque roadway which runs through the Canadian province of Nova Scotia.

The trail measures 298 km in length and completes a loop around the northern tip of the island, passing along and through the beautiful Cape Breton Highlands. The trail passes through many breathtaking scenery and the unforgettable hospitality of many communities. Visitors visiting the trail should take time to go for whale watching, visit the museums and galleries and taste some of the finest sea food in the world.

314 Calakamul

Set deep in the tropical forest of the Tierras Bajas of southern Mexico, **Calakmul**, is an important Mayan site. It is also called the 'City of the Two Adjacent Pyramids'. When the Mayan Civilisation was at its peak, the city probably had a population of 50,000 people! Out of 6750 ancient structures found at this ancient site, the largest is the great pyramid. The city is also known for its murals. Calakmul was designated a UNESCO World Heritage Site in 2002.

315 Cape Canavarel

The City of **Cape Canaveral** is located on the Atlantic Ocean. It stands approximately midpoint between Miami and Jacksonville. This 1.9 square-mile beach is bordered on the west by the Banana River, on the north by Port Canaveral, on the south by Cocoa Beach and on the east by the Atlantic Ocean.

Near to the northern side of the Port Canaveral is the John F. Kennedy Space Centre, NASA. Again, 11. 2 km to the south of the City, lies the Patrick Air Force Base. This strategic location makes the city the centre of America's space activities.

316 Chrysler Building

The **Chrysler Building**, in midtown Manhattan, New York City, was the world's tallest building until the completion (1931) of the Empire State Building. It was designed by William Van Alen, and built between 1926-30. The Chrysler comprised of 77 storeys. It is topped by a series of shining, gradually diminishing arches covered in stainless chromium-nickel steel. The building also exhibits several designs like an enormous stylized eagle heads, pineapples, and automobile-related designs.

317 CN Tower

The **Canadian National Tower**, popularly known as CN Tower, is the world's tallest free-standing structure. It is located in Toronto, Canada. The purpose of constructing the tower was to improve television reception. Approximately 2 million visitors each year come to visit the CN Tower. Though the tower primarily functions for radio and television signals, it also has quite a few attractive features for tourists. At the top of the tower is a revolving CN Tower restaurant which offers excellent view of the surrounding area.

318 Empire State Building

The **Empire State Building** is a 102-storey tall skyscraper located in Midtown Manhattan in the New York City. It was constructed in 1931. It stood as the world's tallest building for 40 years, until the completion of the North Tower of the World Trade Centre in 1972. The Empire State building has two observatories—one is on the 86th floor, the other on the 102nd. The top of the Empire State Building is brightly lighted up at night in dazzling colours to celebrate various holidays.

319 Golden Gate Bridge

The **Golden Gate Bridge** is in San Francisco, USA. It is one of the finest examples of advanced technology. When the bridge was completed in 1937, it became the world's longest and the tallest suspension bridge.

This unique bridge was designed by an engineer called Joseph Strauss. The bridge is 1280 m long, is suspended from 2 cables hung from towers 227.3 m high.

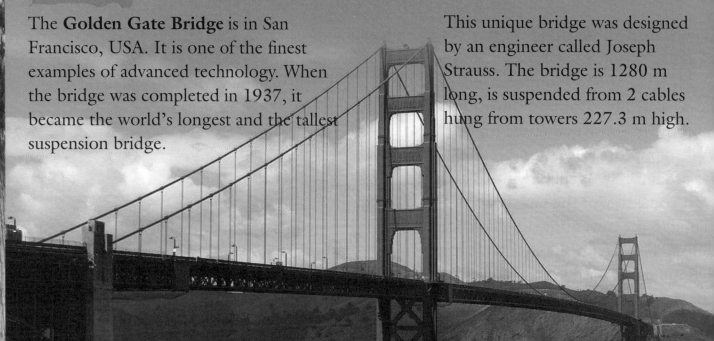

320 Hoover Dam

The **Hoover Dam**, which was previously known as the Boulder Dam, is built on the Colorado River at the Arizona-Nevada border. In 1947, it was renamed to honour President Herbert Hoover. Standing at more than 220.98m above the Colorado River, Hoover Dam is the highest dam in the western hemisphere! It has the world's largest hydroelectric power generating system producing 4 billion kilowatts of electricity every year! Besides all this, the Hoover Dam provides irrigation water to the neighbouring agricultural areas and helps in controlling floods in the area too.

321 House on the Rock

The **House on the Rock** is a huge complex with many rooms which are theme based. These rooms are full of creepy dolls, statues, automated musical instruments, décor with Christmas themes and dusty, broken knick-knacks of all kinds. This might just be America's strangest attraction.

The bizarre house sits on Deer Shelter Rock, a natural column that's 60 ft tall. The House on the Rock is also home to a 200 ft model of a fanciful sea creature, a huge collection of Santa Clause figures and many and many more exhibits. New attractions are continuously being added.

322 Kansas City Public Library

The State Library of Kansas which has a very different and unique look is located in the State Capital building in Topeka. A portion of this library exhibits a book shelf which displays the spine of 22 popular books! This 'Community Bookshelf' is a striking feature of Kansas City's downtown. The impressive bookshelf runs along the south wall of the Central Library's parking garage on the 10th Street between Wyandotte Street and Baltimore Avenue.

323 Kennedy Space Centre

NASA's **Kennedy Space Centre** in Florida has served as America's spaceport for long. It has hosted all the government's manned spaceflights since the late 1960s. The Kennedy Space Centre is located on the Merritt Island, Florida, northwest of Cape Canaveral on the Atlantic Ocean. The centre was named after President John F. Kennedy, who had confidently declared globally in 1961 that the United States would put an astronaut on the moon, and bring that person safely back to Earth too! This declaration succeeded when Neil Armstrong and his two Apollo 11 crewmates splashed down in the Pacific Ocean on July 24, 1969.

324 Las Vegas

Going to **Las Vegas** is a wonderful experience for everyone. It can be fun, romantic, or adventurous as the tourist wants it to be. The city of Las Vegas is located in southern Nevada near the Colorado River. It is the largest city in the state and is the gambling capital of America. There are no clocks inside the casinos, but just never-ending buffets and ever-flowing drinks. Entertainment never ends here but your money may!

325 Lunenburg

The old Town **Lunenburg** is the best existing example of a planned British colonial settlement in North America. The town of Lunenburg was established in 1753 and since then it has retained its original appearance. The townspeople have preserved for centuries the wooden architecture of the houses and public buildings. Wood remains the principal construction material. The architectural plan of Lunenburg's Old Town is remarkably uniform and adhesive.

326 Metropolitan Museum of Art

The **Metropolitan Museum of Art** popularly called 'Met' is one of the world's largest art museums situated in New York. It houses 2 million works of art, covering a period of 5,000 years of world culture, from pre-history to the present day. This vast collection is divided into 19 curatorial departments responsible for specialized collections like the *American art, European art, Egyptian art, Islamic art, or Asian art.*

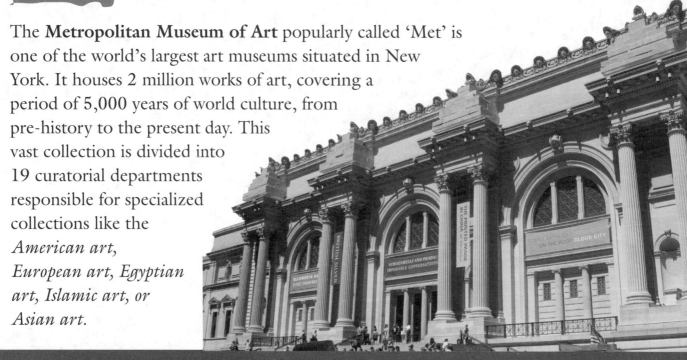

327 Mt. Rushmore National Memorial

Mount Rushmore National Memorial is a huge, awe striking mountain sculpture of the four U.S Presidents. It is located near keystone in the black hills of South Dakota. The Presidents depicted on this unique rock-cut structure are George Washington, Thomas Jefferson, Theodore Roosevelt and Abraham Lincoln. It is said that the 4 heads of Rushmore represent the nation's *independence, democratic process, leadership in the world affairs* and *equality.* Each sculpture is 60 ft tall.

328 Museum of Anthropology

The **Museum of Anthropology** which was founded in 1949 is located within the University of British Columbia, Canada. This anthropological museum houses some 36,000 ethnographic objects and 5,35,000 archaeological objects!

The museum's collection includes contemporary and traditional arts from all continents. The museum's Great Hall displays massive totem poles, carved boxes, bowls, and feast dishes.

329 Museum of Modern Art

The **Museum of Modern Art** is in New York City in the United States. It was established in the late 1920s, by three progressive and influential patrons of the arts, Miss Lillie P. Bliss, Mrs. Cornelius J. Sullivan, and Mrs. John D. Rockefeller, Jr. These patrons felt the need to establish an institution devoted exclusively to modern art. They also felt the need to challenge the conventional museums. And thus, The Museum of Modern Art was established in 1929. The public's response was overwhelmingly enthusiastic. It has the finest collection of modern art including Van Gogh's *Starry Night, Girl before a Mirror* by Picasso, *The Dream* by Rousseau, and many more.

330 New York Skyline

The skyline of New York is one of the world's most recognizable, exhibiting marvels of architecture, historical landmarks and some of the tallest buildings man ever created! Apart from the well-known Empire State and Chrysler Buildings, New York's skyline displays many equally recognizable structures like the triangular-shaped Flatiron building, Hearst Tower, GE building and countless others.

331 Panama Canal

The **Panama Canal** is a 77 km long international waterway that connects the Atlantic and Pacific oceans. It cuts through a narrow strip of land in Panama, a country of Central America. Before the construction of the Panama Canal, ships travelling between the east and west coasts of North America had to go all the way around South America. The canal has shortened the trip for about 14,800 km!

332 Pentagon

Pentagon, the headquarters of the U.S. Department of Defense, is a large five-sided building in Arlington county, Virginia, near Washington, D.C. It was constructed between 1941–43, to consolidate the offices of the War Department. The Pentagon has five floors, excluding its mezzanine and basement. It consists of five concentric pentagons, with 10 spoke like corridors connecting the whole. Pentagon is one of the world's largest office buildings. It is virtually a city in itself. Approximately, 23,000 employees, both military and civilian work there!

333 Sears Towers

Sears Tower is a skyscraper office building in Chicago, Illinois. It was one of the world's tallest buildings. It has a total height of 442 m. It took three years to complete the construction of this tall tower.

The Sears Tower was the world's tallest building until 1996 until Petronas Twin Towers in Kuala Lumpur in Malaysia was constructed.

Sears Tower ⟶

334 Statue of Liberty

The **Statue of Liberty** in New York was a gift from the people of France to the people of the United States as a token of friendship to celebrate the centenary of American independence in 1886. The statue forms a universal symbol of freedom and democracy. The statue was crafted by the French sculptor Frederic Auguste Bartholdi in collaboration with French engineer Gustave Eiffel (of Eiffel tower fame). It is a hollow structure made out of thinly pounded copper sheets over a steel framework. The statue is 46.2 m high. Visitors climb 354 steps which is equivalent to 22 storeys to look out from 25 windows in the crown!

335 Taxco

Taxco is a charming colonial town nestled in the mountains of Guerrero state between Mexico City and Acapulco. The town is charming with winding cobblestone streets and whitewashed houses with red tile roofs, and its impressive Santa Prisca Cathedral.

The town is Mexico's silver capital as it has wealthy deposits of silver. The Silver Museum has an array of silver objects, such as earrings, necklaces, and many other items that have magnificent designs.

336 Tenochtitlán

Tenochtitlán is an ancient city in the central valley of Mexico. It was the capital city of the Aztecs built on a marshy island in Lake Texcoco. The central part of Tenochtitlán was walled and had an enclosure meant for religious activity, containing the main temples of Huitzilopochtli, Tlaloc the Rain God, and Quetzalcóatl. The city also had schools and priests' quarters, a court, and many memorable sculptures.

337 Teotihuacan

48 km north-east of Mexico City lies the ancient city of **Teotihuacan**, one of the oldest known archaeological sites in Mexico. This city which was built between the 1st and 7th centuries A.D. has vast sized monuments like the Temple of Quetzalcoatl and the Pyramids of the Sun and the Moon. They even had hieroglyphics, a calendar, and knowledge about astronomy and herbal medicine! Teotihuacán was designated a UNESCO World Heritage site in 1987.

338 Uxmal

Uxmal, is a ruined ancient Maya city in Yucatán state, Mexico. It is about 150 km west-southwest of Chichén Itzá. Uxmal was designated a World Heritage site in 1996.

The ruins of Uxmal clearly depict that at that time Mayan art and architecture had reached its pinnacle. The three related towns of Kabáh, Labná and Sayil clearly show the social and economic structure of late Mayan society.

339 Walt Disney World

Walt Disney World is a recreational resort owned by the Walt Disney Company in Orlando, Florida. The resort was inaugurated in 1971 with just Magic Kingdom theme park. This amazing resort spreads over an area of 30,500 acres containing 4 theme parks, 2 night-time entertainment area, over 20 hotels, 6 golf courses and much more. Outdoor recreation activities like hiking, biking, boating and swimming are available. It also has four different areas containing shopping, dining, entertainment and nightclubs. It is said that 48 million visitors make the trip to this unique theme park each year!

340 Amazon Rainforest

The **Amazon Rainforest**, also known as the Amazonia or the Amazon Jungle, is the world's largest tropical rain-forest. It covers five and a half million square kilometres! About 60% of the rainforest is within Brazil, 13% in Peru and some parts lie in Colombia, Venezuela, Ecuador, Bolivia, Guyana, Suriname and

French Guiana. The Amazon is over half of the planet's remaining rainforests.

These forests are a home to about 2.5 million types of insects, tens of thousands of plants, 3,000 types of fish, 1,294 types of birds, 427 types of mammals, 428 types of amphibians, and 378 types of reptiles have been identified. The diversity of plant species here is the highest on Earth.

341 Angel Falls

Angel Falls is the world's highest waterfall, with a height of 979 m and the longest uninterrupted drop of 807 m. The waterfall drops over the edge of the Auyantepui Mountain in the Canaima National Park in Venezuela. They are about 20 times higher than Niagara Falls.

The waterfall was named after Jimmie Angel, a US pilot who was the first to fly over the falls in a plane.

The water of the falls appears to be coming from a flat-topped plateau called Auyan-Tepui, which means 'Devils Mountain'. The fall is so tremendous that people walking within a radius of 1.6 km may get sprayed with mist during certain times of the year.

342 Cerrado Protected Areas

Cerrado is one of the world's oldest and most diverse tropical ecosystems located in Brazil. The region is one of the most spectacular high alpine landscapes in the world. This World Natural Heritage Site has an exceptional record of how glaciers and mountains are formed, and also of the effects brought by climatic change. It is also an important cultural landscape. Particularly since its UNESCO extension in 2007.

343 Galapagos Islands

The **Galapagos Islands** are like jewels of the natural world. It is located along the equator, off the west coast of South America.

The Galápagos Islands are an archipelago of volcanic islands. This archipelago consists of 13 major islands, of which 5 are inhabited. The islands are famous for their vast number of endemic species and rich flora and fauna. Numerous scientists and travellers have admired and studied this. The famous British Naturalist Charles Darwin's observations on this island contributed to the inception of Darwin's famous *Theory of Evolution by Natural Selection.*

UNESCO declared the Galapagos Islands a Natural Heritage of Mankind site.

344 Gran Salar de Uyuni

The **Gran Salar de Uyuni** in southwest Bolivia stretches more than 10 square kilometres and is the largest salt flat. It is situated at an altitude of 3,653 m above sea level. It looks more like a desert than a lake.

The flat, pristine white landscape causes optical illusions and reflects colours. There's an island where a giant cacti has grown in the middle of the salt lake.

345 Harbour of Rio de Janeiro

The **Harbour of Rio de Janeiro** is located on the south-western shore of Guanabara Bay. It is surrounded by the city of Rio along a strip of land between the Atlantic Ocean and the Sugar Loaf Mountains, Corcovado Peak, and the hills of Tijuca. The harbour was formed as a result of the eroding action of the Atlantic Ocean along the coast. Rio de Janeiro is the capital city of the State of Rio de Janeiro, the second largest city of Brazil.

The Guanabara Bay is the largest bay in the world based on the volume of water. Rio (or the Guanabara Bay) bay is a natural wonder because of its scenic beauty and the illusions the place produces when one looks at it.

346 Iguazu Falls

Iguazu Falls is a waterfall system of the Iguazu River located on the border of the Brazilian State of Paraná and the Argentine Province of Misiones. The falls consists of 275 falls along 2.7 km of the Iguazu River. *The Devil's Throat*, a large U-shaped waterfall 82 m in height, 150 m in width and 700 m in length is the most impressive of all.

Iguazu offers stunning views and beautiful walkways. At a particular spot a person can stand and be surrounded by 260 degrees of waterfalls! The falls divide the river into the upper and lower Iguazu.

347 Lake Titicaca

Lake Titicaca lies on the border of Peru and Bolivia. It exists 3,811 m above sea level. Lake Titicaca is one of the largest lakes in South America by volume. It is also the highest commercially navigated lake in the world. It is the home to indigenous people like Aymara and the Quechua.

Lake Titicaca is fed by rainfall and melting glaciers. Five major river systems feed into Lake Titicaca. The lake has 41 islands, some of which are densely populated. Lake Titicaca holds large populations of water birds also. Many threatened species such as the huge Titicaca Water Frog and the flightless Titicaca Grebe are largely restricted to this lake.

348 Perito Moreno Glacier

The **Perito Moreno Glacier** is a glacier located in the Los Glaciares National Park, Argentina. It is the world's third largest reserve of freshwater. This glacier gets its name after the explorer Francisco Moreno, who studied the region in the 19th century.

The end of the Perito Moreno Glacier is 5 km wide. Its average height is 74 m above the surface of the water of Lake Argentino. It has a total ice depth of 170 m. It is growing everyday.

349 River Amazon

The **Amazon River** flows for 6437.4 km from the Andes to the sea, and is the second longest river in the world. It is also the largest in terms of the size, the number of tributaries, and the amount of water discharged into the sea. No bridge crosses the river along its entire length. It flows through countries like Peru, Brazil, Venezuela, Ecuador and Bolivia. The majority of this mighty river runs through rainforests rather than roads or cities.

There are over 3000 known species of fish that live in the Amazon River. The largest snake the Anacondas lurk in the shallow waters of the Amazon Basin. The Amazon River is also home to the piranha, a meat eating type of fish who attack their prey in large shoals!

Tierra del Fuego, is an archipelago, at the southern extremity of South America. It is separated from the mainland by the Strait of Magellan. It consists of one large island, five medium-sized islands, and numerous small islands and islets. The total area of this archipelago is 73,746 square km.

The physical features of Tierra del Fuego are varied. Most of the northern portion of the main island consists of glaciers, lakes and moraines. The archipelago was discovered by the navigator Ferdinand Magellan in 1520, when he sailed through the strait. From that time, the strait was named after him and the region was called Tierra del Fuego (Land of Fire). The roads are all in poor condition in Tierra del Fuego, and there are no railways. Air services however, connect the major places.

351 Ariel View of Rio

Rio de Janeiro popularly referred to simply as *Rio*, is the capital city of the State of Rio de Janeiro. The city was the capital of Brazil for nearly two centuries. The geographical setting of Rio makes it one of the most beautiful cities that ever were! It is on a strip of Brazil's Atlantic coast, where the shoreline is oriented east–west. The city was founded on an inlet of this stretch of the coast. The southern part of the city, reaches the beaches fringing the open sea. Rio when seen from the top looks incredible with its golden beaches, the blue waters and the picturesque shoreline.

352 Chickén Itzá

The ancient Maya ruins of **Chichén Itzá** are located on Mexico's Yucatán Peninsula. It is one of the most popular tourist destinations of the world. The ruins contain the remains of many fine stone buildings. The buildings of Chichén Itza are grouped in sets. The best known of these complexes are the Great North Platform. This includes the monuments of El Castillo, Temple of Warriors and the Great Ball Court.

353 Choquequirao

Choquequirao is an old ruined Incan City in southern Peru. It is very similar in structure, architecture and size of Machu Picchu.

In order to come to Choquequirao from the tiny town of Cachora, one has to trek for 20 miles. The surrounding area is an arid land full of cacti until the vegetation turns lush.

354 Easter Islands

Easter Islands is an isolated volcanic island located in the heart of the South Pacific. Its first inhabitants were Polynesians. Their traditions and beliefs led to the carving of the stone statues for which Easter Island is now famous for. Most of the statues are 5.5 to 7 m tall, and a few are shorter than 3 m.

The island was first discovered in 1722, on an Easter Sunday (hence the name), when the Dutch explorer Jacob Roggeveen chanced to have arrived there. Soon, the tales of this exotic island with over 1,000 megalithic statues spread all over the world.

355 El Mirador

El Mirador is a large pre-Columbian Mayan settlement in modern Guatemala. This 'less-known' Mirador Basin which was hidden among a jungle is 2,000 years old. It is often called the Cradle of Maya Civilization. Its five Maya cities, El Mirador, Nakbe, Xulnal, Tintal and Wakna are each larger and older than the nearby Tikal which is far more famous! Among their amazing innovations are super-sized temples and pyramids, including La Danta, the largest-known pyramid in the world and the remains of the world's first highway system.

356 Machu Picchu

Machu Picchu, nestled in the middle of a tropical mountain forest in Peru, belonged to the mighty Inca Civilization. It is also counted among one of the new Seven Wonders of the World. It is often referred to as 'The Lost City of the Incas'.

In modern times, it was discovered in 1911 by Hiram Bingham, a Yala University professor. The primary buildings of these ancient ruins are the Intihuatana and the Temple of the Sun. It was designated a UNESCO World Heritage Site in 1983.

www.toddadams.ne

357 Statue of Christ the Redeemer

Christ the Redeemer is a huge statue of Jesus Christ at the top of Mount Corcovado, Rio de Janeiro, in southeastern Brazil. This unique statue was completed in 1931. It is 30 m tall and it stands with its hands outstretched as if welcoming all. Escalators and elevators were added so that people could reach the statue itself. In 2006, to commemorate the statue's 75th anniversary, a chapel at its base was constructed to *Our Lady of Aparecida*, the patron saint of Brazil.

358 Temple of Kukulkan

The **Temple of Kukulkan** is the most well-known part of the ancient Maya ruins at the famous site of Chichén Itzá. It is often referred to as 'El Castillo' (the castle). This step pyramid has a ground plan of square terraces with stairways going up from each of the four sides to the temple to the top. On the whole, the temple has 365 steps—one for each day of the year. Each of the staircases on the four sides has 91 steps, and the top platform makes the 365th. This glorious step pyramid shows the accuracy and importance of astronomy of the Mayans. The Mayas were so advanced in their astronomical skills that they could even predict solar eclipses!

359 Tikal

Tikal, the ancient Maya city is located deep in the heart of Guatemala's El Petén rainforest. The most important structures in existence at the site are the Temple of the Jaguar, the Temple of the Mask, The Lost World Pyramid, The Great Plaza Ballcourt, Bat Palace and many Altars. Tikal was added to the list of UNESCO World Heritage site in 1979.

360 Aurora Borealis / Australis

Aurora, also known as northern and southern (polar) lights or aurorae, is a natural display of coloured lights in the sky usually observed at night on both the southern and northern hemispheres. It appears as a rippled curtain, pulsating glob, travelling pulse, or a steady glow of colourful light in the sky. It is seen in colours as different as blue, violet, red, ruby, bright green and yellow. The phenomenon occurs at higher altitudes with its lower most ends at 90 to 112 km above the surface of the earth. **Aurora Borealis** is the name given to the aurorae occurring in the northern hemisphere. Aurora that is seen in the southern hemisphere is called **Aurora Australis**.

361 Bermuda Triangle

The **Bermuda Triangle** or the Devil's Triangle is a mythical section of the Atlantic Ocean roughly bounded by Miami, Bermuda and Puerto Rico where countless ships and aircraft have disappeared. No explanations have been found in most of these accidents. The disappearances are still shrouded in mystery. Boats and planes have seemingly vanished from the area in good weather without even sending out messages of anxiety. Although, there are plenty of fanciful theories regarding the Bermuda Triangle, none of them prove that the mysterious disappearances occur only in this part of the globe or more so here, than other areas. In fact, people sail through this area every day without any occurrences.

How the Bermuda Triangle Works Location

Washington, D.C.

USA

Bermuda

Miami

Gulf of Medico

BAHAMAS

San Juan, PUERTO RICO

CUBA

Atlantic Ocea

MEXICO

Caribbean Sea

Map not to scale. For illustration purpose

362 Mariana Trench

Located in the Pacific Ocean, east of the 14 Mariana Islands near Japan, the **Mariana Trench** is the deepest part of the earth's oceans. It is the deepest location of the earth itself. It was created by ocean-to-ocean subduction. Subduction is a phenomena in which a plate topped by oceanic crust is pulled beneath another plate topped by oceanic crust.

'The Challenger Deep' within the Mariana Trench is the deepest known point in Earth's oceans.

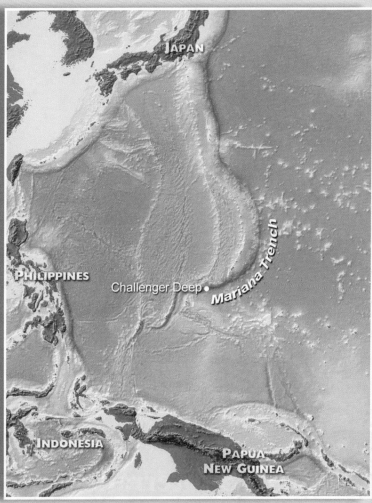

363 Mid Ocean Ridge

Mid Ocean Ridge is the longest mountain range on Earth. It runs over 65,000 kilometres around the globe!

This long range of mountain consists of thousands of volcanoes or volcanic ridge segments which erupt from time to time.

This under-sea system of mountains and valleys criss-crosses the globe. It resembles the stitches in a baseball. About 90 per cent of the mid-ocean ridge system is under the ocean. It's formed by the movement of the Earth's tectonic plates.

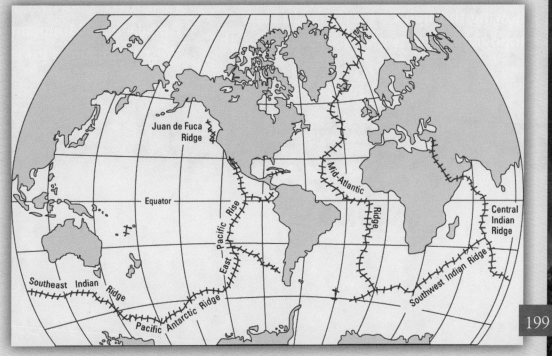

364 Sinkholes

A natural hole that is formed on the Earth's surface as a result of the chemical weathering of carbonate rocks is called a **sinkhole**. Sinkholes vary in size. They can range from 1m to 300 m in diameter and depth. The formation of sinkholes can be gradual or sudden without warning. Sinkholes can be found all over the world and recently large ones have opened in Guatemala, Florida and China. Sinkholes are sometimes called sinks, shake holes, swallow holes, swallets, dolines or cenotes depending on the location.

365 Subterranean River

A **subterranean river** is a river that flow wholly or partially below the ground surface. Rivers that flow in gorges are not grouped as subterranean rivers.

Such rivers maybe entirely natural, flowing through cave systems. In karst topography, rivers may disappear through sinkholes, continuing underground. In some cases, they may appear into daylight further downstream. Fishes such as the Amblyopsidae are adapted to life in subterranean rivers and lakes. The Lost River a 50.1 km long river in the Appalachian Mountains of Hardy County in West Virginia is a good example of this.